Feng Shui
From the Inside, Out

Rev. Victoria Pendragon, D.D.

OZARK
MOUNTAIN
PUBLISHING

For permission, serialization, condensation, adaptions, or for our catalog of other publications, write to Ozark Mountain Publishing, Inc., P.O. box 754, Huntsville, AR 72740, ATTN: Permissions Department.

Library of Congress Cataloging-in-Publication Data

Pendragon, Victoria. – 1946

Feng Shui From the Inside, Out by Rev. Victoria Pendragon, D.D.

This book merges tenets of basic Feng Shui with the Sleep Magic technique to assist the reader in being able to fully realize the results of properly balanced Feng Shui.

1. Feng Shui 2. Metaphysics 3. Sleep Magic

1. Pendragon, Victoria 1946 II. Feng Shui III. Title

Library of Congress Catalog Card Number: 2015936350

ISBN: 9781940265094

Cover Design: noir33.com

Book set in: Calisto MT

Book Design: Tab Pillar

Published by:

PO Box 754

Huntsville, AR 72740

800-935-0045 or 479-738-2348 fax: 479-738-2448

WWW.OZARKMT.COM

Printed in the United States of America

Table of Contents

Introduction   i

1: The Bagua   1

2: Sleep Magic   7

3: Life Path (Point of Consciousness)   10

4: Inspiration/Connection   18

5: The Body/Health and Well-Being   29

6: Sustenance/Finances   41

7: Recognition   57

8: Relationship   70

9: Recreation and Rejuvenation   100

10: Resources   113

11: Combined Baguas   120

12: Creating Your Own Sleep Magic Assignments   125

13: Detailing   132

14: The Ego Process and the External Observer   138

15: The Two Most Critical Rooms in Your House   144

16: Sleep Magic for the Advancing Soul   152

17: Space Clearing   158

18: Detailing the Self   162

In Conclusion   216

About the Author   217

Introduction

In 1995, just after a friend who'd been to a weekend workshop on Feng Shui made a few changes to my townhouse, all of a sudden—out of nowhere it seemed—my then husband finally decided what it was that he wanted to do with his life. "This is amazing," I thought. I had a healing practice back then, and I always had my eye out for efficient ways to assist people in attaining a more comfortable life. Easy has always been important to me; life is difficult enough as it is.

Ten years, numerous certifications, and hundreds of consultations later, by then the owner of my own school for training professional consultants, I was so discouraged with what I was seeing in the lives of my clients that I walked away from a very lucrative practice because I had come to realize that the most powerful Feng Shui of all couldn't be addressed by moving furniture or changing paint color; it wasn't quite as simple as it had once seemed to be on the surface because what I discovered through experience and actual practice was that Feng Shui—the energy of the environment—is not generated solely by the earth, what is built upon it, and how that space is decorated, but also by the inhabitants of the space. I had come to learn, through what would otherwise be called successful results, that when a person is not prepared for those results, the success is fleeting. I also came to discover that it isn't just the space that nurtures the people living and working there, the people affect the space as well.

It all comes down to energy... because everything does. If life were mathematics—and some say that it is—then energy would be the lowest common denominator. In the world of metaphysics, this physical life is often referred to as an illusion; in the world of science, it's called plasma. From either viewpoint you can see the same thing: the inherent potential

i

for change in the so-called physical world because of its energetically flexible nature, especially in conjunction with the power of self-awareness.

Likewise, from a metaphysical/spiritual standpoint, it has also been said that you create your reality and to a degree you do, but the phrasing of that statement is misleading because it makes it sound as if creating your reality is entirely up to you. The fact is that we *co-create* our realities. Just look around; you can't escape it. You are not alone. You cannot hope to manufacture a successful business or profession all by yourself out of thin air and whatever you are thinking; you require people to supply what you need to do what you do as well as people to market to—a counselor needs both training and clients; an author needs both supplies and readers; an artist needs supplies as well as collectors.

Even your very personal little corner of reality—your body—is a co-creation. Who you are now is the result of all the people that have ever touched your life, if only momentarily. Even when you were being carried in your mother's belly, who you are was being unconsciously crafted by everyone with whom your mother came in contact. You know what you know, but you don't know what you don't know and, contrary to a very popular aphorism, what you don't know actually *can* hurt you or can, at the very least, hold you back from realizing your full potential.

This book will present you with the opportunity to allow your self-awareness to expand as you learn a technique that will, if exercised on a daily basis, permit you to free yourself from undesirable emotional/feeling information that lies hidden within the cells of your body, feeling information that generates very low vibration. You will also have the opportunity to begin shifting not only your vibration—and therefore what you draw to yourself—but also the vibrational level of the space in which you live. Co-creation, like everything else, starts at home; your body is your primary home. You will begin to be able to *feel* how it is that what is inside you matters every bit as much as what is around you.

Contrary to what you hear around you almost daily, just changing the way you think cannot generate truly profound change in your life... unless you happened to be 100% ready for that change; and being 100% ready starts, not in your thoughts, but in the countless cells of your body where an entire history of information on what life is all about lives. Why do you suppose the self-help sections of bookstores are jammed with hundreds upon hundreds of books that attempt to teach ways to guide the mind to lead the way to a better life? It's not just because everyone resonates differently with different authors, it's because using your mind to break free of your energetic, emotionally based past is like using a spoon to open a can. In most instances, it can't be done.

Energy psychologies, on the other hand, work beautifully... but the vast majority of people who truly need vibrational change aren't in a position to pay for the years of therapy that it would take to become as clear as a person can become using the technique this book will introduce you to. They aren't able to afford it because unconscious information they carry within is not attracting to them what they need. Sleep Magic, the technique you will be introduced to in this book, is a method that you can use first to raise your vibration to a level that will attract to you a comfortable life and that you can use to continue improving yourself as a more fully self-aware and conscious human being.

You will also learn some of the basic tenets of good Feng Shui for your living space as I present to you a very different way of looking at the bagua, the eight-sided map of spaces that can be used as a guide to object and image placement, a look at color and the influences of the directions on your living space, and explore the dynamics of the two most energetically critical rooms in your house: the kitchen and the bedroom. This down-to-earth approach to Feng Shui will support your personal changes just as the changes you make in yourself will charge your space with vibrant, clear energy.

My second husband—the one who suddenly knew what he wanted to do with his life—ended up bankrupting us ...

twice. He wasn't ready for the opportunity that Feng Shui had brought to him. If you don't shift inside, the outside doesn't make much difference at all.

Welcome to Feng Shui from the Inside, Out.

Basics

Feng Shui, literally translated as Wind Water, is a poetic term for the energy of any environment, inside or out. The earth is alive with energy, an energy that is inescapable and exceedingly obvious in places where volcanic activity is active or where earthquakes happen frequently. Less obvious in places where nature's dirt and rocks have been paved over or neatly reframed into housing plots or farms, the earth's energy is ever present and equally unavoidable in the form of winds, waters, and electromagnetic flows both around and within the earth. These various flows are the most dramatic influencers of Feng Shui, hence its name.

There are other energetic sources that affect earth Feng Shui as well. The sun, the moon, and the stars are the most common of these and can dramatically affect both internal and external Feng Shui. Think for a moment about the ways in which a temperate sunny day affects people or how most people respond to a week of nonstop clouds and rain. Less visually obvious but every bit as profound in its effect are solar flares. We can't see them with the naked eye, yet they wreak havoc with all of our electronic communication devices, generously adding to the frustration levels of helpless users, creating a compromise to the Feng Shui of the spaces in which those people reside or work.

Have you ever been in a room where the tension was so thick you could cut it with a knife? That is external Feng Shui generated by people themselves and a good example of how we affect the spaces we inhabit. There are spaces between the cells of everything; nothing is truly solid. We may perceive things as solid because the cells are so densely packed together but everything is, essentially, plasma. That means that when someone emotes—sends an emotion out into the space that surrounds them—which we do unintentionally all the time, even if we never open our mouths—that emotion, that feeling vibration, is absorbed by the surrounding things, and it adds to the hidden Feng Shui of the space.

The point is, we matter. So much of Feng Shui—wind, water, sun, electromagnetic energy—is out of our hands—that merely rearranging the top of your bureau isn't going to make a huge difference in your life, but transforming yourself into the person who goes *with* the energetic flow, the person who is unaffected by the vagaries of GPS function in a solar storm or by being stuck in traffic for two hours will indeed transform your life, allowing you to become a very living example of good Feng Shui. Once that happens, what occurs on the top of your bureau may affect your life in unexpected and delightful ways.

We'll approach your spaces from an energetic standpoint, a bagua standpoint (more on that later), a directional standpoint, and a psychological standpoint, allowing you to be just as thorough as you want to be with the transformation of your external space. Information on internal and external Feng Shui will alternate and intertwine, just as it does in real life.

Good Feng Shui starts at home, inside you. The changes you make in your space will *support* the changes you make inside, but they can't *make* them happen. Only you can do that. So each chapter's offering will be concluded by a Sleep Magic assignment to help you on your way. All you need to do is read the assignment because your body remembers everything you have ever seen, heard, touched, tasted, smelled, read, felt, and it will easily recall these respectful, humble requests, designed to make its life, as well as yours, easier.

Sleep Magic is designed to touch every waking aspect of your life, the same facets of living that are addressed in Feng Shui through the device of an imaginary map that is laid over any given space, a map called the bagua. If you've been exposed to Feng Shui in the United States then you've no doubt heard a phrase like *relationship corner* or *money corner*. These terms are slight misnomers as corners often have little or nothing to do with the area in question, but never mind that, the concept that lies behind the bagua is that from a given vantage point, different parts of a room—or house or property—relate to different parts of life.

In the compass school of Feng Shui these aspects of life would be assigned to different directions—north, south, etc.—and addressed accordingly. In the early days of the psychological school the bagua was quite confusing as it would inevitably have the word "north" hovering over what was the entry position to any space, a vestigial remnant of its compass origins. Over the years, any reference to actual compass directions fell away and the device became much easier to comprehend.

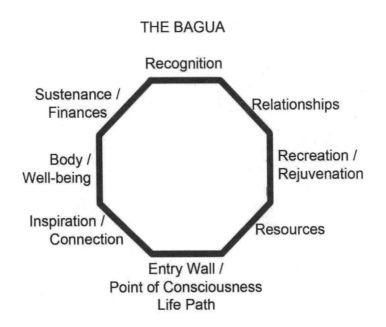

THE BAGUA

Recognition

Sustenance / Finances

Relationships

Body / Well-being

Recreation / Rejuvenation

Inspiration / Connection

Resources

Entry Wall / Point of Consciousness Life Path

The basic understanding of the bagua begins with the Entry Wall/Point of Consciousness. The entry wall to any space is the wall where the door to the space is. In the case of rooms with more than one entry, it would generally be considered to be the door most frequently used although if more than one door is frequently used, each wall can be considered an entry wall, and the bagua map can be laid out in each direction, overlapping itself just as it will in any room where, in addition to the door leading into the space, there are also areas where people spend a large portion of time. We'll address that in detail in a later chapter.

The power of the Entry position is the power of the first impression; the power of a Point of Consciousness—a place where someone may be spending a large amount of time, such as a desk, a bed, couch, or chair—is the power of time itself and the constant exposure it brings to the space viewed from that particular vantage point. Most bedrooms will have overlapping baguas.

Generally, the purview of each of the eight sections of the bagua is about one-third of a flat wall or one-third of each wall when the area takes in a corner of a room.

Life Path / Point of Consciousness: *relates to the life itself as well as to the profession, job, or career of the person/s occupying the space.*

Inspiration / Connection: *relates to what might be called philosophical or spiritual sustenance.*

Body / Well-Being: *relates to general health.*

Sustenance / Finances: *relates both to whatever financial support is currently available as well as to that which might be available for future use.*

Recognition: *relates not just to being acknowledged as existing but to being "known" or appreciated as well, though not necessarily in a public way.*

Relationships: *all types of relationships are covered here, personal, professional, casual, intimate, familial.*

Recreation / Rejuvenation: *often associated with vacations and/or retirement, this area of the bagua has to do with making sure that work is balanced with appropriate rest and time for pleasure.*

Resources: *associated with learning, teaching, mentoring, and being mentored and with travel as a source of broadening one's horizons.*

If you can either copy this page or recreate a bagua for yourself from it, I recommend printing out two baguas on transparent film so that you can lay them out—one over the other, if necessary—on top of a sketch or diagram of your entire living space as well as over each individual room, with the exception of the bathrooms. This will allow you to effectively locate which areas of your rooms fall under the given headings of the bagua.

Working with just one bagua lined up with the entry wall will likely only work well in a space such as an entry hall where, for the most part, traffic moves through the space and does not linger for more than a minute or so. In most rooms you will have areas defined by at least two positionings, giving you such combinations as Relationship/Finances area or Life Path /Resources area. This only makes sense as life is not actually divided up neatly with one part of it in one pocket and another elsewhere; life is interwoven and overlapping, as is our consciousness. Addressing that through the use of multiple transparent baguas makes the pairings fairly obvious. Later on we will go over how that might play out from the standpoint of decorating or accessorizing.

Your body, by the way, is taking all this information in, and even though you may think that this is a lot of information, your body has it all and will be holding it for you. For tonight, we'll give your body the opportunity to clear away more old programming, to assist you in making space.

As I am reading this, I allow myself to feel gratitude for all the many ways you help to keep us comfortable and functional.

I notice how you are feeling and give you permission to relax as we read this, allowing these words to deeply penetrate your consciousness.

Now I picture myself asleep in bed tonight, knowing and understanding that you, my beloved body, will take over and put these words into action for me as I am sleeping, that I need to do nothing more than finish reading this.

I know that you know that we are taking in a lot of information, information that will come in very handy as we transform our life. So I give you permission now to release whatever may seem right and appropriate to you in order to allow us to absorb this information effectively and efficiently.

I honor you for helping us to have the best life of which we are capable.

2
Sleep Magic

Your body knows everything that you have ever seen, heard, smelled, tasted, touched, or otherwise experienced. Ask any forensic hypnotherapist and they'll tell you, people know things they don't know that they know. And while most of us have been trained to think of our brains as the repository for memories, in fact, every cell in our body is filled with memories.

It is this vast repository of cellular memory that stands between us and what we might consider to be an absolutely perfect life. Is having an absolutely perfect life even possible? Yes, it is. Because an absolutely perfect life does not refer to a life where nothing ever goes wrong; it refers to a life in which we are content, in which we can honestly say, at the end of the day, "another perfect day," and mean it because we have come not *only* to understand that life is perfect just as it is but because we are able to embrace life … just as it is. This is where Sleep Magic, the "inside" part of Feng Shui from the Inside, Out, fits into the picture.

Sleep Magic is a do-it-yourself technique for defusing all the low-vibrational, mostly unconscious memories that your body is carrying. How do you know if your body is carrying low-vibrational memories? Well, pretty much everybody is because it simply can't be helped. The first few years of our lives when we have little or no say in what is happening either to or around us are some of the most productive years for laying down what could be called emotional programming in our cells. In the first four years of life (plus the time spent in utero) our brain is creating neural connections at a rate that it will never again come close to. Most of who we think we are is laid down in those first four years and nine months of our lives.

Notice that I say "who we think we are." Those words were carefully chosen because all the neural connections made during that time were based on the needs of an infant body working to survive in a world where it had no control, a world of massive external input where the major role for any little body is to be a sponge. Most of us spend a lifetime discovering who we *really* are and many never get there. Time and adult experiences can never outweigh that initial emotional input but can, given enough time, dull its effect. Sleep Magic speeds up that process by decades through allowing the body to let go of old and outdated information that it has carried for a lifetime, enabling you not just to dull the effect but to generate a higher vibration.

Just as no space that is cluttered can be said to have good Feng Shui, no person who is carrying the luggage of their unconsciously lived early years can be said to have good internal Feng Shui. Consequently, no matter how perfectly balanced the living space, if the person living within the space does not meet its high standards, the results will be less than spectacular. It's rather similar to applying paint to a surface that has not been properly prepared.

The assignments you will receive at the end of each chapter are designed to allow your body consciousness to release unconscious emotional programming. By the end of a month in which you do Sleep Magic nightly, your body will have experienced this process through every phase of the moon and because your body is a creature of habit, if you continue practicing Sleep Magic, in the following month your body will become more and more comfortable with the process, allowing it to deepen its trust. With each passing month that you utilize the technique, your body will be able to release from deeper and deeper levels.

Because your body remembers everything, it will remember the following assignment as you read it and will, per the instructions that are built into it, set everything in motion once you have fallen asleep. All you have to do to make it work is read it. This assignment marks the beginning of a new, productive, and very intimate relationship with your body as well as the first step to improved vibration.

*[Do only one Sleep Magic assignment per night. It's not respectful of the body to ask for too much all at once. So, if you have just read the assignment from Chapter One, bookmark this page for the following night.]

As I am reading this, I allow myself to feel gratitude to you, my body, for all that you have done for me throughout the course of this day.

I notice how you are feeling and give you permission to relax as we read this.

I picture myself asleep in bed tonight, knowing and understanding that you, my beloved body, will take over and put these words into action for me as I am sleeping, that I need to do nothing more than finish reading this.

I know that you know everything I have ever heard, tasted, smelled, felt, seen, and thought. Tonight we are going to begin to work together in a new way. Tonight I am going to ask you to be my helper and my teacher. I am going to ask for your help to become everything that you know I came here to be.

So tonight, to the degree that it is comfortable for you, I give you permission to release whatever we need to release to begin this journey together. You can fill the empty space its leaving creates by expanding what ability I have to form habits that work in my behalf.

I thank you for working with me to become everything that I came here to be.

Sweet sleep!

Life Path (Point of Consciousness)

Feng Shui

What I refer to as the Life Path section of the bagua is oftentimes referred to as the "career" area, a term I find to be far too limited for the scope of this portion of the octagon, which covers, essentially, what it is that you do in the world. Not everyone has a career, but everyone has a Life Path.

The Life Path region is associated with the entry wall of a room but can also be tied to any area of a room where you spend a great deal of time. When sitting at your desk, for instance, the chair in which you sit can become your Life Path, the rest of what may well be a very small bagua rolling out in front of you, with your keyboard residing in the center and, following your direct line of vision, whatever is across from you becoming the Recognition area, and so on. Your chair becomes a Point of Consciousness.

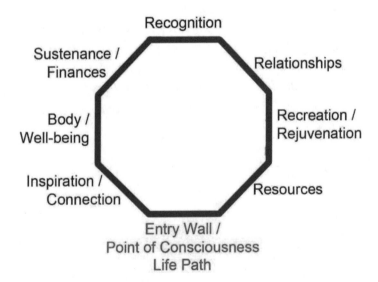

This particular orientation puts a great deal of pressure on you to have excellent, supportive seating because who doesn't want to feel supported on their Life Path? The same applies to your bed. Yes, you may be more or less unconscious while you're in it, but the fact that you are not aware of the influences going on around you as you sleep does not lessen their effect on your physical body, especially in those particularly vulnerable times just before falling asleep and waking up when your mind is especially open.

If you are wondering, "Well, if the Life Path area is my bed, what about my door?" The simple answer is that the Entry Wall of your space is always going to be a Life Path area. So, yes, there may be more than one Life Path area in your room ... and all the others areas of the bagua as well. In fact, that will be the case in many rooms where regular seating—or sleeping—takes place. And just to complicate matters, in situations such as dining rooms or living rooms or dens, where many people have regular sitting areas, each person will have his or her own bagua in addition to the overall bagua of the entire room.

So, no, it's not simple, but it's not really all that complicated either; there are just a lot of things to consider in certain rooms when it comes to the very particular part of Feng Shui that relates to the way in which images affect the psychology of the people viewing them. For the most part, though, when people are seated in their Life Path area as a Point of Consciousness area, at a desk, for instance, or watching TV, their backs are to the area itself, thus the effect of imagery in a Point of Consciousness area itself is of little importance because that imagery will be behind the person and mostly unseen so you can pay more attention to those areas in front of them and to the parts of the bagua they represent.

As a general rule, images that might imply danger, sadness, death, or fear have no place in a home. That said, these sorts of images are often irresistible to teenagers and their rooms are the exception to almost every rule of Feng Shui. In fact, it's best just to stay out of them, something that is often particularly difficult for parents to do. Aside from the occasional check for possible health hazards (which should be announced ahead of time), it is usually best, from a psychological standpoint, to avoid trespassing in teenage-claimed territory because that's exactly what it is: territory.

Teenagers are on a Life Path that is all their own. Their brains are awash in hormones as are their bodies, and they have every reason to want to be left alone. Providing them with a home steeped in good energy and showing them support while exercising common sense and consistency as far as house rules go is the best you can do for them and for the atmospheric Feng Shui of your home.

The Life Path area has traditionally been associated with the element of Water, which is why you often see aquariums, usually near the door, in Chinese restaurants. When translating the element of Water to your home you can do the same if you are so inclined, although please keep fish bowls out of the bedroom! The only living creatures—in an adult bedroom—should be the adults themselves. You can be more lax with this for children as their bedrooms are very much the only part of the world that they can lay claim to and they need to have some sense of their power so some peaceful fish near the door would be fine. (No fighting fish or piranhas, please!)

Blue, white, or clear glass is the obvious way to reference the element of water when you want to enhance a Life Path area. Art glass is wonderful as are cut flowers in a vase, but cut flowers anywhere in the home must be carefully attended to and must look fresh and perky at all times if you want to be Feng Shui compliant because practically nobody's subconscious likes to be reminded of a slow death.

In summary, when addressing Life Path areas think *support* if you are seated and references to water and flow for imagery and decoration. An image of a mountain stream might well provide both elements ... but only if the scene is one that truly moves you. Ideally, every image or piece of art in your home means something to you, generating good feelings whenever you see them, which makes excellent Feng Shui!

Sleep Magic

Some people seem to be born knowing exactly who they are and exactly what they want to do in the world; for others, it's just not that simple. Some folks never really find a job they love or work they can commit to ... that's human nature. We aren't all designed to be the same. Our challenge is to find out what makes us content in life and usually that comes with accepting who we are and how we are in the world. This is one of the reasons to ensure that the Life Path areas in your home reflect back to you the concept of being supported so that you can more easily go with the flow of life.

At certain times in our lives it may be that the control that we think we should be able to exercise over our lives is compromised, as when we are young and subject to our parents' rule, or if we are chronically sick, infirm, or disabled. At those times it is especially useful to have symbols of support around us, to remind us to go with the flow, to allow us to resonate with the strength that we carry within ... but sometimes it is difficult to connect with that inner strength, to remember that there is always support for us. At those times, Sleep Magic can come in especially handy.

Giving your body permission to let go of its despondency, to release whatever it is that you have been carrying with you that has allowed you to feel hopeless or worthless or dejected or even angry can lighten the stress on your body and soul as well as your mind. Any healthcare professional will tell you that attitude in healing makes all the difference in the world, and any mental health professional will tell you that attitude makes all the difference in life, period.

13

Some of us carry inborn chemistry that causes us to be more down than up, but recognizing that for what it is—biology—can make a difference in how we handle the down times. Sleep Magic can help with that as well. Although it cannot necessarily change your body chemistry, it can help you deal with it. Giving your body permission to release whatever it needs to let go of in order to allow you to both see and accept yourself without judgment will help you to be more gentle with yourself, smoothing your path. An assignment like this could help:

As I am reading this, I allow myself to feel gratitude for all the many ways you help to keep us comfortable and functional.

I notice how you are feeling and give you permission to relax as we read this, allowing these words to deeply penetrate your consciousness.

Now I picture myself asleep in bed tonight, knowing and understanding that you, my beloved body, will take over and put these words into action for me as I am sleeping, that I need to do nothing more than finish reading this.

I know that you know that I feel down a lot and I know that you know, too, what is behind that. Feeling down feels as if it holds me back.

So I give you permission now to release whatever seems right and appropriate to you to let go of so that I can feel more light and lifted up.

Thank you for helping me to be comfortable with who I am.

The Life Path can also relate to careers and jobs and professions, even to landing a job. Inside of most of us there lives an ideal sense of what it is that we'd like to be doing with our lives. When that's there, inside, it's as if we have an on-board compass that we can follow, guiding us to where we need to go to get what we want. But for some, the compass seems faulty, leading to dead ends and disappointments. And for others it's as if life never gave them even a clue about what might make them feel fulfilled. Still, in every one of us, there lives a part that *does* know, all we need to do is to access it. Sleep Magic can assist you in doing just that.

I refer to that innate source of wisdom as Spirit or the Divine. It feels to me as if it is the force that animates my body. I don't even pretend to know what it is or where it comes from, but naming it makes it easy to refer to it, so I do. And I need to refer to it because that innate source is the wisdom that your body has access to via Sleep Magic, when your mind and your Ego Process are fast asleep. The following assignment could help someone who was casting about for something to do with his or her life:

As I am reading this, I allow myself to feel gratitude for all the many ways you help to keep us comfortable and functional.

I notice how you are feeling and give you permission to relax as we read this, allowing these words to deeply penetrate your consciousness.

Now I picture myself asleep in bed tonight, knowing and understanding that you, my beloved body, will take over and put these words into action for me as I am sleeping, that I need to do nothing more than finish reading this.

I know that you know that I have been searching for right work, for something to do that feels right for me.

So I give you permission now to release whatever seems right and appropriate to you to let go of so that I can be open to your wisdom, so that I can attract to me the opportunities that are trying to find me.

Thank you for helping me to feel more and more like myself all the time.

These assignments, because they are constructed in such a way as to give your body the comfort it deserves, can unfold slowly sometimes, so if you need them, you may want to do them once a week or so—no more than that—allowing your body to feel safe, to trust you to allow it to change at its own rate. Know that your Life Path is exactly as it should be at every moment and commit to working with your body so that you can go with the flow you're in.

Assignments for the Life Path Area of Life

As I am reading this, I allow myself to feel gratitude for all the many ways you help to keep us comfortable and functional.

I notice how you are feeling and give you permission to relax as we read this, allowing these words to deeply penetrate your consciousness.

Now I picture myself asleep in bed tonight, knowing and understanding that you, my beloved body, will take over and put these words into action for me as I am sleeping, that I need to do nothing more than finish reading this.

I know that you know our Life Path even better than I do, and it would be useful for me to have access to your wisdom so I give you permission now to release whatever seems right and appropriate to you to let go of so that we may expand our openness to your innate knowledge of what we are here to do in the world.

I honor you for helping me to be the best me I can be.

Untapped Gifts and Potential

As I am reading this, I allow myself to feel gratitude to you, my wonderful body, for everything you do for me every day, breathing, circulating my blood and lymph, allowing the food I eat to nourish me, protecting me.

I notice how my body is feeling right now.

Now I picture myself asleep in bed tonight, knowing and understanding that you, my beloved body, will take over and put these

words into action for me as I am sleeping, that I need to do nothing more than finish reading this.

I know that you know that we hold within us gifts that we have not yet realized. To the degree that it is comfortable for you and appropriate for us, I give you permission to release whatever may stand in the way of those gifts ripening, expanding, and becoming more useful to us.

In the morning I will take note of how I feel. Thank you for helping me to be all that I can be!

Inspiration/Connection

Feng Shui

Energy in interior spaces flows clockwise from the main entry door so we will make our way around the bagua in a clockwise fashion also, going with that flow. This leads us then to the area of Inspiration and Connection, that is, to the area that resonates with whatever it is that feels like our source, whatever it is that we rely on for inspiration or that feels as if it connects us to the rest of humanity/the earth/the universes. Some people might see this area as their God or religion area. Others, less spiritually inclined, might interpret this area as having to do with nature itself. It's a space that is very personal in nature.

If you are in bed or at your desk or seated somewhere, this area—like the Resource area directly across from it—will be at least partially unseen by you, but it will be available to your peripheral vision and will be at least partially seen whenever you look in that direction. The fact that this area becomes almost secondary in your visual awareness speaks to how easily this aspect of your life can be forgotten, especially when the mind is overwhelmed or the heart is hurting, the times when you most need it.

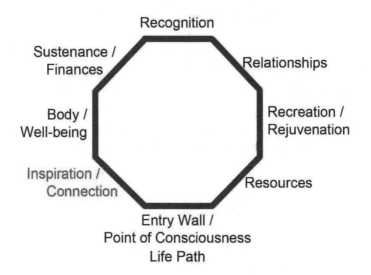

A bedroom is an especially good place to address this area well precisely because of the openness of the body to influences when it is sleeping. Just to the left of the head of your bed, if you are lying on your back, this area, like the Life Path area directly behind you and the resource area on the right side of the bed, provides a sense of support, in this case the support of the unseen, the support of that which you cannot ever really know yet are somehow aware of it, a sense, perhaps, of the energy of Life.

The element of Earth is associated with the area of inspiration and connection although it is not the deep, rich soil that yields the abundance of plants that fuel our lives, it is rather, mountain-like earth, hard and craggy, untamed, unplowed, virgin, sometimes challenging life itself. It represents the energy that *leads* to beginnings, it is the uncracked seed, newly dropped, called to burst forth by forces beyond its own scope or control. Inspiration is, after all, very much like a seed, no more than a thought passing through your mind until you make it real through your own efforts.

Some people, like me, are given to create altar-like spaces where they gather meaningful items together to display them, items that tie them to memories, places, people,

19

and items that connect them to the larger web of existence in some way. These things carry an emotional energy that lends them power, binding the mind, the heart, the soul to what may have been only a fleeting moment, the very stuff of inspiration. The Inspiration / Connection section of the bagua is an excellent place for such a display, a perfect place to drop anchor while activating the energy of the area as well.

This is the place of what might be called wisdom. I have heard wisdom defined both as "the heart informing the mind" and "experience merging with intuition." It is both, I imagine, and more, born of awareness, mass consciousness, and a shared, seemingly infinite intelligence that we can never claim as "belonging" to anyone.

Sleep Magic

Spirit and body have a sort of a contract. You have no doubt heard it said that we pick our parents. In doing so, we pick our bodies too. It's logical when you think about it. The body you inhabit is integral to the nature and the passion and the desires of your spirit.

Your spirit is the essence of you. It is what makes you, *you*. Spirit, as I am using the term, is a metaphor for the infusion of whatever energy you think, feel, or believe is generating the universe. Your spirit is part of that. As are all spirits. And all spirits are different. We are, taken as a whole species, like facets on an immense diamond, each of us reflecting the light in our own way.

Spirit is here for the party. And, at the spirit level of being, it's all a party. Because spirit is pure energy and energy just is. Energy, despite what you may have heard colloquially, is neither good nor bad. It is just that we, as humans, tend to qualify everything. So we qualify energy too. But as spirits, all we do is *experience* energy. As humans, anger is a very unpleasant way to experience energy and we tend to call

20

it "bad." Spirit doesn't. Spirit eats it up. Why? Because anger is just another way to experience energy and spirit is here *to* experience.

Some spirits are more adventuresome than other spirits. Some spirits want to be on the fast track. They want to cram as much learning into one lifetime as they can. Those spirits will inevitably choose a life of high energy. It might be the high energy of an abusive childhood or the high energy of a serious drug addiction or the high energy of deep-sea diving or teaching in a high-risk school system. Whatever type of life experience it is that spirit has picked, it has done so for its own reasons.

Other spirits are more easygoing. Their idea of learning may take the form of everyday accidents and job-hunting issues. We are all spirits in this material world and we are all different. And, bottom line, it is Spirit that runs the show. If you have spent your whole life feeling sorry for yourself because you've had such a hideous life, you might want to consider looking at it from another perspective, the perspective of "what on earth could my spirit have been thinking?" You may just get some answers that way that can allow you to view your life from an entirely different vantage point and that can only be helpful because it has been scientifically proven that it is not our genetics that shapes our lives, nor is it our environment per se that shapes our lives. It is, rather, our perception of our environment that shapes our lives.

That's a very spiritual scientific conclusion, but Dr. Bruce Lipton lays it out point by point in his book, *The Biology of Belief*. It's a heavy book, complex in the science it is teaching, but the conclusion is as simple and elegant as any mathematical proof. What you think affects what happens to you.

Spirit is in charge. Your job and my job are to figure out, if we don't already know, what Spirit is up to. The sooner you can make peace with the passionate force that is the Spirit moving your life, the sooner you can open up to that particular flow in the stream of passion. When people speak of "coming to peace" with the life they have lived, it is the Spirit level of their being with which they have come to peace. Once you have come to peace with the needs and desires of your Spirit, you get to experience passion because Spirit *is* passion.

If you have a sense of who you are in the world, then you are connected. Connected to what? you might ask. Connected, in a broad sense, to Life itself, to the Ubuntu—the energy of humanity. If you feel that connection then you are comfortable in your own skin most of the time yet sometimes even the most-grounded individual, comfortable in his or her own skin, can feel somewhat unconnected, a little lost. It is at times such as that when pictures and objects that inspire you come in very handy, serving to remind you of who you are.

But that very centered sense of self is something that each one of us is born with. We come into this world with a great deal of energetic integrity ... but we also come into this world still very much attached to the energy of our mothers and we stay very much a part of her energetic field for many years if she is present. In ancient Chinese medicine when a child under seven years of age was ill, it was the mother who was treated.

Young children who are deprived of their mothers as infants or young children may end up with somewhat less of a sense of being supported in the world. This often manifests as issues with weight or with money. Being a part—*feeling* a part, both physically and energetically—of a nurturing, caring, larger being adds dramatically to a sense of security that stays in place throughout the life.

If you have struggled, either with your weight or with money, it may, energetically, relate to the first years of your life and the physical and/or emotional availability of your mother. Sleep Magic assignments give your body permission to release whatever lies behind those issues, allows it to expand the energy around a time when you may have experienced a sense of being truly supported, can help move you into having more and more of that inner sense of support.

Likewise, if you have issues with self-confidence, you can look to your childhood relationship with your father. Unlike our mothers, whose energy is literally a part of us and our energy a part of her, our fathers have a choice in the matter and their attention and love, given freely, begrudgingly, or withheld sculpts our sense of what we are worth.

Pre-birth programming and that from infancy and early childhood, up to about age four, has special sticking power because those are the years of the greatest production of neural connections. The information we take in during that time, pretty much unconsciously because at that point in development we have no internal censors, no way to close off our minds, is then supported by all the years that follow in which the information is passed down in the cellular memory of the body. It is information that most people have no knowledge of, yet it is there, at work, inside you, and your life is the reflection of it. Where you are dissatisfied with yourself, you will find the material you need, through Sleep Magic assignments, to change yourself.

Sleep Magic assignments can assist you in regaining the self-confidence that is your birthright by giving your body permission to let go of feelings of worthlessness or doubt and replacing them by expanding the energy around some time when you felt really and truly good about yourself, no matter how short the time may have been or how seemingly insignificant the happening.

The more you become clear, free of old programming that has little to do with you, the more you begin to real-ize yourself. When thinking of art or images that you might want to have around you, try to begin thinking in metaphorical terms, thinking of yourself, perhaps in terms of what animal or flower or tree seems to you to reflect qualities that you value in yourself. For instance, a young therapist I once worked with imagined herself as an ancient oak with a broad trunk and roots that sank deep into the ground, allowing the branches of the canopy to spread wide, providing homes and shelter for animals and people alike. Unable to locate an actual photograph of her magnificently imagined tree, she had one drawn for her. She used this image to activate the energy in the Inspiration / Connection area of her personal office.

Assignments for the Inspiration/ Connection Area of Life

The following assignment is meant simply to align you with your body's wisdom:

As I am reading this, I allow myself to feel gratitude for all the many ways you help to keep us comfortable and functional.

I notice how you are feeling and give you permission to relax as we read this, allowing these words to deeply penetrate your consciousness.

Now I picture myself asleep in bed tonight, knowing and understanding that you, my beloved body, will take over and put these words into action for me as I am sleeping, that I need to do nothing more than finish reading this.

I know that you know our Life Path even better than I do, and it would be useful for me to have access to your wisdom so I give you permission now to release whatever seems right and appropriate to you to let go of so that we may expand our openness to your innate knowledge of who we truly are.

I honor you for helping me to be the best me I can be.

This assignment is useful for people with confidence issues as such folks often give themselves far less credit than they deserve and, in doing so, tend to accept lower value for their work.

As I am reading this, I allow myself to feel gratitude to you, my wonderful body, for everything you do for me every day, breathing, circulating my blood and lymph, allowing the food I eat to nourish me, protecting me.

I notice how you are feeling and give you permission to relax as we read this, allowing these words to deeply penetrate your consciousness.

Now I picture myself asleep in bed tonight, knowing and understanding that you, my beloved body, will take over and put these words into action for me as I am sleeping, that I need to do nothing more than finish reading this.

I know that you know that I have a tendency to undervalue both myself and the gifts that I have. To do so, I know, renders us both a disservice. So I give you permission now, to the degree that you are comfortable, to release whatever is creating that mode of behavior.

You can fill any empty space that may be created by expanding the feelings I have when I recognize the talented person that I truly am.

I honor you for helping me to love myself more and more every day.

The next assignment will dive deep, back into your pre-birth days, to release a little more of what you may possibly still unconsciously be carrying around. If the possible scenario never happened then the assignment is neutralized, the body simply ignores it because all the body knows is what is; negatives do not exist for it.

As I am reading this, I allow myself to feel gratitude to you, my body, for all that you have done for me throughout the course of this day.

I notice how you are feeling and give you permission to relax as we read this, allowing these words to deeply penetrate your consciousness.

Now I picture myself asleep in bed tonight, knowing and understanding that you, my beloved body, will take over and put these words into action for me as I am sleeping, that I need to do nothing more than finish reading this.

I know that you remember growing inside our mother's uterus. I know that you know that we were nourished there on everything she held inside her and some of those things were not so good. I give you permission now to release any feelings of stupidity that may have come into us from growing inside our mother and to fill the empty space by expanding the feeling of validation I had one time when I realized that I had been right about something.

Thank you for helping me to find greater peace of mind.

Opening to Spirit Self

I notice how my body is feeling, and I am grateful to it for supporting me in every way.

I picture myself asleep in bed tonight, knowing and understanding that you, my beloved body, will take over and put these words into action for me as I am sleeping, that I need to do nothing more than finish reading this.

I know that you are fully aware of my Spirit Self and that I can be more fully open to my Spirit Self by being more fully open to your consciousness. So, to the degree that it is comfortable for you, I give you permission to release anything that stands in the way of my being conscious of the information that you have for me.

You can fill the empty space its leaving creates by expanding our communication.

I thank you for working with me to become everything that I came here to be.

Why I Am Here

As I am reading this, I allow myself to feel gratitude (for something, anything).

I notice how my body is feeling.

Now I picture myself asleep in bed tonight, knowing and understanding that you, my beloved body, will take over and put these words into action for me as I am sleeping, that I need to do nothing more than finish reading this.

I know that you know why we are here on Earth. I know that you know that I don't know. So I give you permission to release whatever you may need to release, to the degree that you are comfortable in doing so, whatever you may need to in order to allow me to be more comfortable with trusting that your knowing is enough.

You can fill the empty space created by expanding the pleasure I feel when I am lost in a good story.

In the morning I will take note of how I feel. Thank you for helping me to be all that I can be!

Alternate Life Resonance

No matter how we may judge our lives to be, we are always exactly where we should be, doing exactly what we should be doing. If you feel out of alignment with your circumstances, it is possible that the area—or one like it—may figure in an alternate lifetime.

The following assignment can prove useful when it seems as if you are simply not in the right place.

Thank you, dear body, for all the work you did for me today. I am so grateful for breathing and for my blood circulating, for digesting food and casting off what we do not need.

As I read this I allow myself to become aware of my breath, of how my muscles are feeling, if I feel limited anywhere in our body or if I feel any pain or discomfort.

Now, I imagine myself getting into bed tonight, getting as comfortable as I can be, feeling myself beginning to relax, knowing that you, my wonderfully hard-working body, will be processing this request for us as we sleep.

I know that you know that at the level of our spiritual DNA we may have spent other lifetimes in this country/area, or one very similar. To the degree that it is possible and comfortable for you, I give you permission to release something we no longer need in order to allow us to more fully feel that resonance.

Thank you for hearing me and for working with me in our behalf. I love you.

The Body/Health and Well-Being

Feng Shui

The bagua is an energetic map of interior spaces that is used in what is often called Psychological School or Western Feng Shui. When Feng Shui began to be widely known in the United States, it was regarded as a kind of manifestation tool, which it simply isn't. Assessing and adjusting Feng Shui is best done with an eye to creating a balanced, healthful life. That's why it goes so well with Sleep Magic, which is all about assessing and adjusting your vibration in order to have a comfortable life, and since the bagua pretty much touches on all aspects of life, you can see yourself reflected in your living space and vice versa.

The bagua, as you follow it around, mirrors many different cycles, among them, the passage of the moon and the sun through the sky, the seasons, and life itself. The Life Path area represents time out of time in the cycle of life, while the area of Inspiration/Connection is similar to conception and fetal growth. In the life of a tree, as in human life, this phase of development takes place unseen; the first real clue we have that something is growing are a few green leaves pushing through the earth. This young tree or sprout energy is the energy of the Body/Well-being portion of the bagua, that insistence on being, on growing, on living no matter what the circumstances. It is pure life force.

It has often been noted in metaphysical circles that of all living things, the energetic configuration of the tree comes closest to the energetic configuration of humans. Although our energetic roots are invisible, we do have them; the root chakra is what connects us to the earth. Like the trees, we stand erect, and like the trees, our energetic crown—the crown chakra which opens up at the top of the head—connects us to All That Is. Like the trees, too, our nourishment is derived from above and below, and is processed in between. It is no wonder, then, that the element of Wood—tree energy—is connected to this area of the bagua.

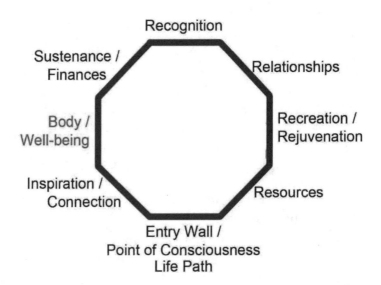

Life force is nothing if not insistent. Infants are sometimes born lacking critical organs, organs that are necessary to life, and yet, even severely compromised, these immature and incomplete bodies will grasp at life. This too is like the trees. I'm sure that you have seen trees sprouting in the most unlikely places: on rooftops where there is no soil at all, on cement walls, on expressways. They may not attain the maturity of a well-placed specimen, but they will live a life where few others might survive. This is what we do as well. In fact, we rely on the resilience of our bodies so much that we tend to ignore their small complaints well past the comfort level of our bodies.

Placed on the center of the wall that is to the left of the Entry Wall, the Body/Well-being facet of the bagua is usually easily seen upon entering a room, yet it is still not front and center as are the three most focused-upon spots in Feng Shui on the wall opposite the Entry. Most of us take our bodies and their functions for granted unless we have been given reason not to. That is why it is so critical to ensure that the energy in the Body and Well-Being area is as good as it can possibly be because it needs to support our body's unconscious drive to live as we, from time to time, ignore or forget about it.

Plants are good for activating the energy in this area if there are windows to provide light … but plants need to be cared for so if that's not who you are and you know darn well that you'll forget to water, go for artwork … or silk plants. I know that gardeners and florists alike balk at the idea of silk plants and flowers, but guess what, the subconscious mind doesn't! The subconscious mind is childlike in nature and takes things at face value. Better a silk plant than a dying one, especially in the Body/Well-Being area of a room.

Also, make sure that any appliances in this area are working as they should. Lights should light. Things that run on batteries should have batteries that work. Anything with moving parts, electrical or not, should work otherwise the subconscious signal that's sent is that something is not working correctly in your body.

Because this area resonates with the energy of young growing trees, light shades of green, similar to the colors of young plants, are especially wonderful in this area, even more so in a bedroom or kitchen, two rooms of the house where the body is nourished. (And green always goes nicely in a bathroom; it's "tree" energy serving to use up all the water that's there.) In ancient China, where the actual compass was used to mark Feng Shui territory, this section of the compass, related to the body and its health was always located in the eastern part of the home and when possible the walls were almost entirely green.

31

Sleep Magic

There's a colloquial saying: if you have your health, you have everything, yet few people seem to value that advice to the degree that would be wise, ignoring the inborn wisdom of their bodies to instead drive themselves relentlessly in pursuit of either money or thrills when, logically, without a healthy body you can truly enjoy neither.

Fact is, most of us have been trained from childhood to ignore our body's voices. What we are trained to do is to be obedient, to follow directions, to do what we are told to do. Every body is different; our internal chemistries vary. At a temperature of 68° you will see adults attired in everything from tank tops to coats yet parents inevitably—and with the best intentions—dress their children either to match their own responses to the weather or to match the internal programming they carry, a gift from their parents when they were young, on what is appropriate clothing. Either way, the child's actual needs are usually ignored.

A child will run out gaily into what seems to be perfectly clement weather wearing the clothes on its back only to be dragged back in and told to "put something on." Thus do we learn to ignore our own thermostats. The same thing happens with food. "Eat that, it's good for you." "Finish what's on your plate." "There are children starving in (currently featured third-world country)." So it's really small wonder that most people glean what become their ideas on health maintenance from magazines, doctors, and other healthcare professionals when everyone's best authority on the general upkeep of their bodies is the bodies themselves.

If only we taught our children to respond to their natural likes and dislikes instead of squashing them in favor of what some authority thinks works best ... oh, wait! We actually *could* do that if we wanted to, and it would work just fine.

Years ago—decades ago, in fact—researchers presented a group of infants with an array of foods on their highchairs from which they could eat whatever they liked. What they discovered was that although on any given day some child might consume only one thing at one meal, by the end of a week every child in the study had consumed what could be termed a balanced diet. Infants' bodies are smart and in control. Most parenting ensures that such inborn wisdom is squashed by so-called reason.

In later years, especially when sports are involved, the body is again subjected to the whims of overzealous coaches and parents as advice like, "walk it off" or "get back in there" is proffered, overriding the body's need to have its energetic flow restored or even just to take a rest. The body even takes a backseat to schoolwork, which must, at all costs, come first, never mind how tired you may be.

What am I getting at? The fact that most of us have a pretty strained relationship with our bodies, and that's not helpful. Your relationship with your body is the most intimate and the most important relationship you will ever have, and chances are good that your body doesn't feel as if it can trust you.

You can start now to fix that relationship by using Sleep Magic to restore trust. That's the thing about Sleep Magic assignments that you may have already noticed: they're all about giving the body permission to do things, about giving it options, letting it decide what is right and appropriate for itself ... and by extension, you, because you and your body are, after all, inseparable.

You can use assignments to find out how your body feels about everything from a supplement you might be considering, to a job offer, to a vacation idea. Because your body knows what is best for it, it knows what is best for you and will happily tell you if you ask.

Your body's information will come to you in its language: feelings. Never mind the story a dream may tell you, the important thing will always be: How did you feel (in the dream or upon awakening)? How you feel is your body's information for you. Feelings are never wrong. If you felt good

33

or happy, your body has given you a thumbs-up. If you felt scared or angry or in any way compromised, that's a no-no for sure. And if you felt perfectly neutral, then whatever it was, it doesn't much matter one way or the other.

As you and your body grow closer through the use of Sleep Magic you will find that, as in any relationship, your communication improves ... in other words, your intuition, which you may think is already pretty darn good, will begin to amaze you. This is Feng Shui from the inside, out, creating your body/mind/soul as a place where you can weather life's storms.

Assignments for the Body / Well-being Area of Your Life

Here's a little something for your body, just to show it that you care:

Thank you, dear body, for all the work you did for me today. I am grateful to you for breathing and for my blood circulating, for digesting food, and for casting off what we do not need.

As I read this I allow myself to become aware of my breath, of how my muscles are feeling, if I feel limited anywhere in our body or if I feel any pain or discomfort.

Now, I imagine myself getting into bed tonight, getting as comfortable as I can be, feeling myself beginning to relax, knowing that you, my wonderfully hard-working body, will be processing this request for us as we sleep.

I know that you would know that we are not always strictly attentive to your needs, and I apologize for that. I'd like to do better, listening to you, paying attention to you.

So I give you permission tonight to release whatever might seem right and appropriate to let go of in order to expand my responsiveness to your needs.

Thank you for hearing me and for working with me in our behalf. I love you.

Loving the Body

As I am here reading this, I feel tremendous gratitude to a wonderful universe that always—and I really mean ALWAYS—takes care of me.

I am aware of my body—my arms, my legs, the way my head is held, the curves of my spine, and the expansion and contraction of my chest and belly as I breathe.

I picture me tonight, in bed, drifting off to sleep, connecting with this moment in time as I am preparing myself for transformation. I know, dear body, that you will assist me in transformation as I sleep.

I know that you know that I am grateful to you for all the work you have done in our behalf. What you may not know is how much I love you. I love you unconditionally, just as you are, and I give you permission to release, to the degree that you are comfortable in so doing, anything that would stand in the way of your feeling that love and allowing it to expand to every cell.

Thank you for your help.

Often, people balk at the use of the phrase, "just as you are," especially when they are not satisfied with "how" they are. But conditional love, while it works well for most adult relationships, is no help to a body that has all the sensitivity of a two-year-old child or a cat or a dog and needs to feel love. If your body is sick or disabled or has been labeled as too heavy or too thin, by you or by others, then it needs all the love you can give it. You wouldn't withhold love from a sick child or a maimed pet … why would you keep it from the unique and precious vehicle that allows you to experience life on earth?

Aligning Body and Spirit

I notice how my body is feeling, and I am grateful to it for supporting me in every way.

I picture myself asleep in bed tonight, knowing and understanding that you, my beloved body, will take over and put these words into action for me as I am sleeping, that I need to do nothing more than finish reading this.

I know that you are fully aware of my Spirit Self and that I can be more fully open to my Spirit Self by being more fully open to your consciousness. So, to the degree that it is comfortable for you, I give you permission to release anything that stands in the way of my being open to the desires of my Spirit.

You can fill the empty space its leaving creates by expanding the clarity of our communication.

WEIGHT ISSUES

Indiscriminate Eating

As I am reading this, I allow myself to feel gratitude to you, my wonderful body, for everything you do for me every day, breathing, circulating my blood and lymph, allowing the food I eat to nourish me, and for protecting me.

I notice how you are feeling and give you permission to relax as we read this, allowing these words to deeply penetrate your consciousness.

Now I picture myself asleep in bed tonight, knowing and understanding that you, my beloved body, will take over and put these words into action for me as I am sleeping, that I need to do nothing more than finish reading this.

I know that you know that I sometimes eat things simply because they are in front of me. I am aware that this activity may prove detrimental if I indulge in it too frequently.

So I give you permission now, to the degree that you are comfortable, to release whatever feels right and appropriate to you in order to expand my conscious awareness of and control over this behavior.

Thank you for helping us both to be more comfortable in the world.

Healing—Assisting the Healing Process

As I am reading this, I allow myself to feel gratitude for everything that you, my beloved body, do for me through the day and the night.

I notice how you are feeling right now, and I give you permission to relax as I read this.

Now I picture myself asleep in bed tonight, knowing and understanding that you, my beloved body, will take over and put these words into action for me as I am sleeping, that I need to do nothing more than finish reading these words.

I know that you would know if there is anything we are holding onto that would slow the process of healing from (the way you currently feel or the condition with which you are dealing). If there is, you have my permission, to the degree that you are comfortable, to release it.

You can fill the empty space its leaving creates by expanding the way I feel when we are at our physical best.

Thank you for helping us to heal.

Please notice the almost interchangeable use of the terms "I" and "we." "I" is usually used when you are interpreting your side of things to the body, but since you and the body exist in the same space, "we" is often applicable. When the body is unwell, "you" feel unwell also. "You" are the experiencer of the body; the body, on its own, just is. So when you are talking about feeling good it may be "you" being able to *observe* that you feel good or it may be you *experiencing* feeling good. When you are referring to the experiencing process, "you" becomes "we."

Four Assignments Dealing with
Familial or Genetic Disorders

Releasing absorbed conversations / infant

As I am reading this, I allow myself to feel gratitude for everything that you, my beloved body, have done for me today.

I notice how we are feeling, right now, in this moment, and I give you permission to relax as we read this, allowing this request to penetrate our cellular consciousness. Now I picture myself asleep in bed tonight, knowing and understanding that you, my beloved body, will take over and put these words into action for me as I am sleeping, that I need to do nothing more than finish reading this.

I know that you know that we may have been exposed, when we were an infant, to conversations about ____ and how it showed up in previous generations. If any of these conversations may have contained information that led us to manifest similar symptoms, I give you permission, to the degree that you are comfortable, to release whatever that information might have been.

I honor you for helping me to be more comfortable with my own biology and to be better able to manage it.

Releasing absorbed conversations / crawling child

As I am reading this, I allow myself to feel gratitude for everything that you, my beloved body, have done for me today.

I notice how we are feeling, right now, in this moment, and I give you permission to relax as we read this, allowing this request to penetrate our cellular consciousness. Now I picture myself asleep in bed tonight, knowing and understanding that you, my beloved body, will take over and put these words into action for me as I am sleeping, that I need to do nothing more than finish reading this.

I know that you know that we may have been exposed, when we were only crawling, in our early years, to conversations about _____ and how it showed up in previous generations. If any of these conversations may have contained information that led us to manifest similar symptoms, I give you permission, to the degree that you are comfortable, to release whatever that information might have been.

I honor you for helping me to be more comfortable with my own biology and to be better able to manage it.

Releasing absorbed conversations / older child

As I am reading this, I allow myself to feel gratitude for everything that you, my beloved body, have done for me today.

I notice how we are feeling, right now, in this moment, and I give you permission to relax as we read this, allowing this request to penetrate our cellular consciousness. Now I picture myself asleep in bed tonight, knowing and understanding that you, my beloved body, will take over and put these words into action for me as I am sleeping, that I need to do nothing more than finish reading this.

I know that you know that we may have been exposed, when we were young, to conversations about _____ and how it has showed up in previous generations. If any of these conversations may have contained information that led us to manifest similar symptoms, I give you permission, to the degree that you are comfortable, to release whatever that information might have been.

I honor you for helping me to be more comfortable with my own biology and to be better able to manage it.

Overheard Conversations, Projections, and Unconscious Determinations

As I am reading this, I allow myself to feel gratitude for all that you, my beloved body, have done for me in the course of the last day.

I notice how we are feeling and I give you permission to relax as we read this, allowing the words to deeply penetrate into our cellular consciousness.

Now I picture us asleep in bed tonight; I imagine us resting comfortably.

I know that you know far better than my current consciousness knows about conversations we may have been exposed to as an infant, conversations that were about the likelihood of my displaying the familial tendency to _____.

If that was the case, and I was exposed to such a conversation or conversations, I give you permission to release any determination of any expectation that I would indeed manifest those tremors as an adult.

You can fill the empty spaces that are created by their leaving by expanding the energy of steadiness that I feel/felt _____.

Thank you for helping me to help us to feel more clear about who we are now.

Withholding love from your body will slow down any healing that you may have had in mind. Don't do it. Your body will work with you, if you will work with your body to establish trust.

Sustenance/Finances

Feng Shui

Directly across from the entry wall is the wall most immediately accessible both to sight and to awareness, the wall where, lined up neatly in a row, we find what seem to be the most demanding of the eight facets of the bagua map: Finances, Recognition, and Relationships. In all my years as a consultant, these three areas were of more concern to more people than any others despite the fact that other areas—Connection and Resources, particularly—would have been of far more use to them since until you master your Self, you are unlikely to do really well at anything else.

Finances are important, of course; we need money—or its equivalent—to live in today's world, so money matters, it is not unimportant. Money is a form of energy; you exchange your "work" to acquire it, expending your energy for whatever amount of money is deemed to be of equivalent value. Attention paid to one's financial well-being is time well spent since there comes a point when your physical energy may be in decline and the vicissitudes of stock market are unreliable at best. Therefore, attention paid to the Finance area of the bagua is equally well spent.

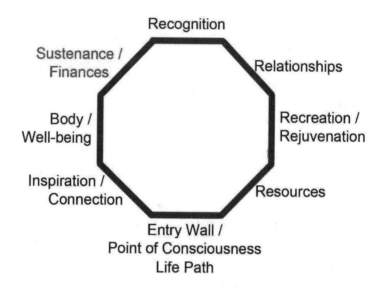

In order to best treat your own particular Sustenance/Finance area, you need to know who you really are because the trappings of good psychologically based Feng Shui are dependent on your own subconscious for fuel. As an example, let's say that while out shopping you came across a gee-gaw of some sort that advertised itself as something to place in your "wealth corner" (a phrase you will never hear me use except in explanation), presumably to bring you wealth. Unless that item took your breath away before you knew what it was for, it's pretty much useless as far as being anything of value to you.

If you purchase that item and bring it home, installing it somewhere in the far left area of a room, every time your subconscious sees it, it will say to itself—and therefore to you—"There's that thing we bought to bring us more money," effectively amplifying the fact that you spent money on something because you need/want more money. It will *not* convey to your subconscious mind what it would need in order to enhance your vibration in such a way that it would draw money to you. For that, what you need is something that thrills you, something that when you see it you are amazed and delighted to remember again that you own it because it is just so precious, just so beautiful, just so astounding. What you need is something that makes you *feel* as wealthy as you think you would like to be.

And guess what, if you start feeling that way on a regular basis, your vibration begins to shift a little (or a lot if you are doing this work in conjunction with Sleep Magic), and eventually it dawns on you that maybe what you have is exactly enough, that perhaps this comfort that you are experiencing is the wealth you truly desire. Free of the desire for "more" you open yourself up to true abundance.

Everyone needs enough money to live, ideally, enough money to be comfortable. No one needs more money than they can actually use. Look to the body for good information on that subject. The body needs food, but too much food and you know what happens. Look to your Sustenance/Finance area as a place where you celebrate what you have and you will find that all your needs are met.

Sleep Magic

While money is important, it is often said that it "can't buy happiness," except that it kind of can. Scientific studies have shown that those who struggle to make a living are significantly less happy than those who don't. But it has also been shown that beyond the point of having a little extra for some little extras and knowing that you'll have something to depend on come retirement time, the happiness quotient doesn't rise at all. Happiness (and is this really a surprise?) is more about having a fulfilling life than it is about having a boatload of money.

Earlier I spoke about the relationship between one's mother and one's finances. Just in case that little piece of information slipped past you, I'll mention it again. If your mother was absent—either emotionally or physically—especially from your first four years—there is some chance that your finances can become an issue because mother = support, and if your body did not experience support in those crucial, neural connection building years, then no-support may become your body's normal, its default, creating a life of not-making-it or just-barely-making-it.

Likewise, if your parents were struggling with money while your mother was carrying you or during your childhood, your body would absorb the information that life is about financial struggle. Bodies can go in one of two directions when they have information like that ... or sometimes, more confusingly, both. They can be driven to make sure that such a thing never happens to them, sometimes working themselves into an early grave or alienating themselves from potential friends because of their obsessive devotion to their work, or they can recreate a similar scenario, unconsciously crafting a life in the same unfortunate mold as their parents. Alternately, they may find themselves veering between the two extremes, seemingly without any control at all over their fortune.

Sometimes, the children of very wealthy families can experience a backlash around money if the family members are mean or worse, associating money with bad behavior and avoiding it at all cost, even if to their own detriment. The results can be very similar to those whose parents struggled.

These misguided scenarios are all fixable. Sleep Magic is one easy way to go, you just need to have patience with the process. Because just as mother = support, money = support and support = survival. Survival is the Primal Urge. If your body has unconsciously linked any of these issues in its life with its very survival yielding serious challenges in its—and your—relationship to money then you must proceed with care and caution, allowing your body to let go of all its old programming at its own speed.

The following assignment is designed for someone who suspects that his or her early childhood might have created a current less-than-desirable financial atmosphere. Because this issue is one that likely runs deep and because you are dealing with the way that your body—a very long time ago—figured out how best to stay alive in the world, you have to be especially cautious about not badgering it by repeating the assignment too frequently, so pay close attention the very first time you do it, to the way you feel either in any dreams that arise or when you wake in the morning.

If you have any negative-feeling responses, wait at least ten days before attempting the assignment again and when you do, be sure to add to the wording that you know that your body knows that the last time you did it, it didn't feel so good. Let your body know that you will be patient with it, that you will give it all the time it needs.

Assignments for the Sustenance/Finance Area of Your Life

Notice the use of phrases like "may have" and "may be" in the body of the assignment; this is because we don't really *know* what has happened for absolute sure, we only *suspect*, so the use of words that leave the door open for the body to fill in the blanks give it some leeway.

As I am reading this, I allow myself to feel gratitude to you, my wonderful body, for everything you do for me every day, breathing, circulating my blood and lymph, allowing the food I eat to nourish me, and protecting me.

I notice how you, my body, are feeling right now, and I give you permission to relax as we read this, allowing the words to sink deep into our cellular consciousness.

Now I picture myself asleep in bed tonight, knowing and understanding that you, my beloved body, will take over and put these

words into action for me as I am sleeping, that I need to do nothing more than finish reading this.

I know that you know that we may have gotten some very (here, fill in whatever descriptive word feels right to you) ideas about money in our childhood, ideas that may be behind the financial struggles we are currently experiencing.

So, to the degree that it is comfortable for you, I give you permission to let go of whatever might feel good and right and comfortable for you to release that would allow us to expand the energy of the way we felt when (here, fill in some time when you actually felt as if you had enough of something good, it could be anything).

Thank you for helping me to work in concert with you for the betterment of our life.

Here's an assignment designed to help you to balance your budget.

As I am reading this, I allow myself to feel gratitude to you, my wonderful body, for everything you do for me every day, breathing, circulating my blood and lymph, allowing the food I eat to nourish me, and protecting me.

I notice how you, my body, are feeling right now, and I give you permission to relax as we read this, allowing the words to sink deep into our cellular consciousness.

Now I picture myself asleep in bed tonight, knowing and understanding that you, my beloved body, will take over and put these words into action for me as I am sleeping, that I need to do nothing more than finish reading this.

I know that you know that the life I am currently living is a good one; it is also demanding. I could use a little more money in my life to balance the budget.

So, to the degree that it is comfortable for you, I give you permission to let go of whatever might feel good and right and comfortable for you to release that would allow me to step into the vibration that would draw those additional funds to me.

Thank you for helping me to work in concert with you for the betterment of our life.

Job

Sometimes it feels as if the job you have is less than perfect. That doesn't necessarily mean that you have to look for another job! It may just mean that you need to use Sleep Magic to release some things you may be carrying inside you. Releasing whatever is behind the things with which you are dissatisfied can allow a shift in your current workplace that may make it just where you want to be.

One by one, make a list of the things you do not like about your current job.

For each thing that you do not like, write an assignment that will allow you to release whatever is behind your being in a job where you have to put up with that.

Fill the empty space with opposite feelings; expand the way you feel when you do things you might already be doing in some other context that you would like to be doing in your job.

You can use this same technique for any situation where you find yourself in a group whose dynamics seem less than pleasant to you.

Attracting a Job

As I am reading this, I allow myself to feel gratitude to you, my wonderful body, for everything you do for me every day, breathing, circulating my blood and lymph, allowing the food I eat to nourish me, protecting me.

I notice how my body is feeling right now.

Now I picture myself asleep in bed tonight, knowing and understanding that you, my beloved body, will take over and put these words into action for me as I am sleeping, that I need to do nothing more than finish reading this.

Dear body, I know that you know how much pleasure we have when we are doing work that we love. I would like to be in a job I loved so that I could experience this every day. So, to the degree that it is comfortable for you, I give you permission to release whatever it is that stands in the way of my being in a job like that.

You can fill the empty space that is created by expanding the pleasure that we have when we are doing a task that we really enjoy.

Thank you, dear body. You are my absolute best friend.

Trusting the Universe

As I am reading this, I allow myself to feel gratitude to you, my wonderful body, for everything you do for me every day, breathing, circulating my blood and lymph, allowing the food I eat to nourish me, protecting me.

I notice how my body is feeling right now.

Now I picture myself asleep in bed tonight, knowing and understanding that you, my beloved body, will take over and put these words into action for me as I am sleeping, that I need to do nothing more than finish reading this.

I know you know what we need to do to allow my consciousness to shift into a place of trust that the universe will bring me what I need in terms of work that will sustain me. To the degree that is comfortable for you to do so, I give you permission to release whatever might be in the way of making that shift (and whatever is behind that or causing it) and to expand the sense of trust I have that the universe will bring me what I need.

You can fill the empty space that is created by expanding the pleasure that we have when we are doing a task that we really enjoy.

Thank you, dear body. You are my absolute best friend.

Food = Survival = Money

If you have problems either with your weight or with money, you have been (notice the past tense) the victim of what I call tainted love. Our mothers are supposed to provide us with nourishment. It is they, ultimately, who govern our relationship to both food and money because it is they who were ultimately responsible (in utero and childhood) for feeding us and for protecting us, hence, for our survival.

In utero we absorb our mother's feelings and her energy. This becomes focused and concretized as subconscious belief systems once we are out of the womb in the words we hear that we may be thought, at the time, to not understand. And, indeed, we may not understand the words, but our bodies remember them nonetheless, as well as the emotion that surrounded them when they were spoken. That energy can also become concretized in us through any food prepared by either parent since their energy goes into the food they are making that we will consume. Some of this can be addressed by going back and doing the in-utero work again, letting go of whatever internalized beliefs your mother may have passed on to you concerning food/money/survival.

A mother's self-worth can also come into play so you might want to repeat the in-utero sleep spell about "self-worth" once every ten days or so for a while if either money or food is showing up as a problem for you because, if your mother's self-worth is an issue, yours—whether or not you are aware of it—may be as well. So I suggest the following Sleep Magic assignment in addition: *"I know that you know that we received little or no support from our parents when we were young. Intellectually I know that effect on me was unintentional and that I had and have value and I need to know that in every cell of my body, so I give you permission to expand that knowingness into every cell of our body and to integrate it into my waking consciousness."*

The next thing I suggest is that you search your body's memory banks for one food that you like the taste of. (Just liking it is enough; *really* liking it would be too much for this particular assignment.) Then, get that food and, at a time when there is nothing to disturb you—turn OFF the phone—sit down with your body and with the food. Hold the food in front of you. Become really conscious of what has allowed it to be there in front of you. Did it have to be planted and tended? Did it have to eat? Did it have to be invented? Who did those things? What was required to get that food to you? Send your gratitude—love, if you can manage it—to the food itself and to every other life form that was involved in getting that food to you. Then, slowly and with consciousness, eat the food. Savor it if you can, allowing the flavor to fill your mouth, allowing some degree of pleasure in the process to reach your waking conscious mind. Then, wash up and remove all traces of the event.

Once you have accomplished that exercise, you can use the experience of it to expand and integrate into the cellular consciousness of your body, allowing your body to begin to feel the benefits of real nurturing. The bottom line is that no one can care for you as well as you can care for yourself. Your body will love you for it and, as time passes, your relationship will deepen. As that happens, the vibration you carry about "having what you need" will expand too. Food and money will begin to fall into place in your consciousness and in your life.

This may mean that you have sudden revelations about money and how you relate to it. Use those revelations to create assignments for yourself where you release whatever is *behind* the feeling or issue. Remember to fill the empty space its leaving creates by expanding an experience of satiety of satisfaction.

Mother's Concerns about Money

As I am reading this, I allow myself to feel gratitude (for something, anything).

I notice how my body is feeling.

Now I picture myself asleep in bed tonight, knowing and understanding that you, my beloved body, will take over and put these words into action for me as I am sleeping, that I need to do nothing more than finish reading this.

I know that you remember when we were in utero that my mother may have had concerns about money. I know that if she did, I may have absorbed those feelings that she had. Such feelings would be detrimental now that I am aware that I create my own reality.

So to the degree that it is comfortable for you, I give you permission to let those feelings go.

You can fill the empty space their leaving creates by expanding the feeling I have when I receive payment in full for a job I have done.

I honor you for helping us to feel secure in the world.

Feeling at Risk

As I am reading this, I allow myself to feel gratitude (for something, anything).

I notice how my body is feeling.

Now I picture myself asleep in bed tonight, knowing and understanding that you, my beloved body, will take over and put these words into action for me as I am sleeping, that I need to do nothing more than finish reading this.

I know that you remember when we were small, the feelings I had that I was at risk, unprotected. That time is long gone and I have created a life in which I am safe. Those old feelings of vulnerability are of little use to either of us.

51

So to the degree that it is comfortable for you, I give you permission to let those feelings go.

You can fill the empty space their leaving creates by expanding the feeling I have when I am snuggled up in bed on a cool morning.

In the morning when I awaken I will take note of how I feel. I honor you for helping me.

Unfulfilled Desires as a Child—Disappointment

As I am reading this, I allow myself to feel gratitude (for something, anything).

I notice how my body is feeling.

Now I picture myself asleep in bed tonight, knowing and understanding that you, my beloved body, will take over and put these words into action for me as I am sleeping, that I need to do nothing more than finish reading this.

I know that you remember when we were small, the feelings I had sometimes when I wanted things and could not have them. Those old feelings of disappointment are of little use to serve either of us.

So to the degree that it is comfortable for you, I give you permission to let those feelings go.

You can fill the empty space their leaving creates by expanding the feeling I have when I receive a gift that I have really wanted or really enjoy.

In the morning when I awaken I will take note of how I feel. I honor you for helping me.

Unfulfilled Desires as a Child—Helplessness

As I am reading this, I allow myself to feel gratitude (for something, anything).

I notice how my body is feeling.

Now I picture myself asleep in bed tonight, knowing and understanding that you, my beloved body, will take over and put these words into action for me as I am sleeping, that I need to do nothing more than finish reading this.

I know that you remember when we were small, the feelings I had sometimes when I wanted things and could not have them. Those old feelings of helplessness work against our sense of well-being.

So to the degree that it is comfortable for you, I give you permission to let those feelings go.

You can fill the empty space their leaving creates by expanding the feeling I have when I make something happen!

In the morning when I awaken I will take note of how I feel. I honor you for helping me.

Attracting More Income

As I am reading this, I allow myself to feel gratitude to you, my wonderful body, for everything you do for me every day, breathing, circulating my blood and lymph, allowing the food I eat to nourish me, protecting me.

I notice how my body is feeling right now.

Now I picture myself asleep in bed tonight, knowing and understanding that you, my beloved body, will take over and put these words into action for me as I am sleeping, that I need to do nothing more than finish reading this.

I know that you know that additional income would be useful to us now and that it would be useful for me to focus on those things that can add to our income so, to the degree that it is possible for you, I give you permission to release whatever you might need to release to expand our ability to attract more money to us.

Thank you, dear body. You are my absolute best friend.

Money—I Have All That I Need

This assignment is valid to use if all your bills are being met, even if just barely because the vibration of your attitude has everything to do with what you attract and you cannot do better than having an attitude that resonates with the abundance of the universe as being something that is always available to you.

As I am reading this, I allow myself to feel gratitude to you, my wonderful body, for everything you do for me every day, breathing, circulating my blood and lymph, allowing the food I eat to nourish me, protecting me.

I notice how my body is feeling right now.

Now I picture myself asleep in bed tonight, knowing and understanding that you, my beloved body, will take over and put these words into action for me as I am sleeping, that I need to do nothing more than finish reading this.

I know intellectually that I have and always will have everything that I need. This is something that I would like to know in every cell of my body so I give you permission to release whatever you may be comfortable with in order to expand this knowingness into every cell of my body to and to integrate it into the cellular consciousness of our body right down to the DNA.

In the morning when I awaken I will take note of how I feel. I honor you for helping me.

When asking your body for information around the energy of something—say, for instance, that you have two or three different job opportunities and you take each one into sleep on separate nights—be sure to go with the feelings that come up and not with the specifics of any dream content that you might experience. That said, if something specific does come up in a dream and you awake knowing fully and immediately what that very specific information is about, trust the knowing. *Knowing* is a feeling. Anything you have to think about ("I wonder if ...") can be let go from your mind as extraneous.

Sometimes, in your waking life, you may experience doubts or anxiety around something. These doubts and anxieties could be your body telling you that something is up, that you had better pay attention, but they could also be old, outdated programming left over from childhood triggering your Ego Process. Sleep Magic can assist you in telling the difference between the two possibilities. Use the following approach:

As I am reading this, I allow myself to feel gratitude to you, my wonderful body, for everything you do for me every day, breathing, circulating my blood and lymph, allowing the food I eat to nourish me, protecting me.

I notice how my body is feeling right now.

Now I picture myself asleep in bed tonight, knowing and understanding that you, my beloved body, will take over and put these words into action for me as I am sleeping, that I need to do nothing more than finish reading this.

I know that you know that I've been feeling _____ about _____ lately. If this feeling is the result of old information that we've been holding onto, and is detrimental to our well-being, I give you permission, to the degree that you are comfortable, to let it go. You can fill any empty space that may be created by its leaving by expanding whatever feels right and appropriate to you.

If, on the other hand, this feeling is coming directly from your wisdom and I should be acting on it in some way, please, to the degree that it is comfortable, release whatever would allow that information to become known to my waking consciousness.

In the morning when I awaken I will take note of how I feel. I honor you for helping me.

The knowingness that you can expect may come at any time but usually it will be at some point within the next day.

It may well come like a bolt of lightning out of the blue when you are engaged in some activity, focused on something else entirely, as if, all of a sudden, you just *know*. Trust the know-ingness.

Remember to base your assignments on things that have caused a level of dissatisfaction or discomfort and not on things you "want" to have happen unless you have already checked with your body to ensure that what you want is what the body wants also. In other words, before creating an assignment to attract something, ask your body what the energy is around that something. If it gives you a positive response, then you can work with it to attract whatever it is to you.

Recognition

Feng Shui

Stars are like diamonds in the night sky ... of course, save for the moon, what else is there to see in the night sky except for stars? Still, that's the word we use to describe those people who seem to outshine the rest of us, whose faces—and more!—become everyday icons. Thanks to the writer's strike in the early 2000s that forced the hand of television producers to find something for us to watch—anything! please!—thus spawning reality shows, and made the idea that anyone can become a star—dare I say it—a reality. The fact is, everyone needs at least a little attention, some, more than others, and to be recognized, to be acknowledged as special, almost always feels good.

In life, we see ourselves reflected physically in mirrors and energetically in everyone we meet; the lives we live are reflections of who we are. If you want to know who you are, all you need to do is look around you. That's why, on the map of the bagua, directly opposite the Entry Wall, in the Life Path area, you find Recognition. It is, in an almost literal sense, in your face: you cannot avoid yourself. So what do you see there?

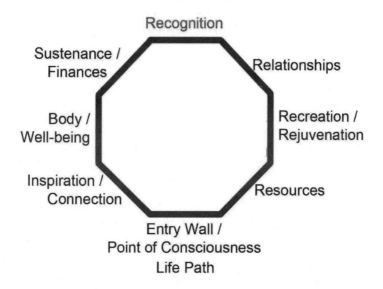

Stroll through your living space and check out what you have hanging or sitting in the very center of the wall opposite the Entry Wall. Reflect a bit on what you see, on what it may be telling you about yourself and, if it seems appropriate, on what might better be in that space.

Remember, too, that across from wherever you spend a lot of time sitting or standing—at your desk, across from the television, in a studio or workspace—there will also be a Recognition area. (And when you sit across from a television, how does what you are watching reflect who you think you are?)

The Recognition area is another great opportunity for metaphorical thinking on how you conceive of yourself. My own desk provides an amusing example of a Recognition area ... this is, apparently, how I see myself at work: There are three Major Arcana cards from three different tarot decks: the High Priestess, the Magician, and Justice. There is an image of a letter, a reminder about clear writing, a reminder that I owe it to the world to write, a small thank-you card (because I am SO grateful ... for everything), a couple of shamanic references, a couple of references to art and being an artist, a butterfly, and a snake (transformation is my middle name), a wolf, my favorite Aura-Soma bottle, and a couple of Mother's Day cards. Behind all that are my most continuously used reference books. That is who I am when I am seated at my computer.

It may not be simple ... but it's effective and at least somewhat attractive. Kind of like me. When I sit down to work here, to write, everything in my Recognition area tells me who I am and what I'm doing here (as if I could forget). It's a thoughtful, potent, powerful—and changing—display for me. Something like this might drive someone else up the wall. How you see yourself—and how you wish others to see you—is a very personal thing and it needs to resonate with you.

In the case of family dwellings or the homes of couples, critical Recognition areas will be the main entry to the living space in the area surrounding the front door of the home and the bedroom/s. For families, the recognition of the whole family is appropriate in shared areas like the living room or the entry itself. Photographs are fine but make sure that they are relatively recent; a photographic history or montage is a wonderful and a fun thing, but do make sure that recent pictures are there as well. This is especially relevant for the parents of grown children. It's lovely that your children were adorable when they were babies, but once they're grown it's important that your offspring have the chance to see that you honor them as the adults they have become.

Children benefit greatly from exceptional shots of them hung across from their beds so that they have the opportunity to resonate with what is best in them on a daily basis. If they play a sport or an instrument, a photo of that would be wonderful. Images of a child engaged in his or her passion feeds that passion. Likewise, if he or she is an artist or musician, an especially good piece or the tools of their chosen art will also help them to form a solid self-image.

The recognition area in the bedroom of a couple ought to feed back to them their sense of two being one. A sculpture of dancers or a couple embracing, as long as it is a relatively neutral piece—not displaying distinct, identifiable facial features—would work well. The twin champagne glasses from a wedding ceremony can be used to create the proper atmosphere. A sculpture of two animals together, relating to each other, carries the perfect sort of relationship energy for the bedroom of a couple.

Recognition areas, in reflecting an idea of who you are back at you, build your internal sense of self, strengthening confidence and comfort in who you are, so chose your images wisely.

Sleep Magic

I am whatever I say I am; if I wasn't then why would I say I am?

—Eminem

We are born, most of us, into an attention-saturated atmosphere; some of us enter the world as if in a spotlight, with the eyes of any number of onlookers on us, and the adoration that most of us receive as newborns is never again equaled, but what a great way to start life!

Except for hermits, almost everyone both wants and needs to be recognized, seen for who they are. In business, it's essential if you want to succeed, and in private life it's usually both desirable and comfortable to be affirmed by others. Recognition is an aspect of attention, but it carries a value that simply getting attention doesn't.

Babies and children supposedly crave attention; I say *supposedly* because, in fact, babies and children both need and deserve attention. Babies and children that don't get the attention that all small living creatures require can go to great lengths to get it ... so can the adults they grow up to be. But that doesn't usually yield the kind of recognition that is useful. Nevertheless, when young human beings are deprived of the attention they rightly deserve, the lack stays with them. If they are smart, they go about filling that void in ways that are socially acceptable and perhaps even useful, but if they have been so injured by careless adults who probably never received the attention they deserved when they were children, that they cannot make sense of the world, then their ploys to attract attention can range from mildly annoying to things that may seem crazy and the recognition they get can sometimes come with jail time.

Happily, the majority of humanity is not so broken but many of us are just broken enough that the vibration we carry draws to us a kind of recognition that we don't necessarily want. The Law of Attraction works like a charm so if you are attracting attention from others who may seem to you to be less than desirable, then you are carrying attractors—almost inevitably from childhood—that are putting out that wavelength. Where the attractors came from doesn't really matter; blaming never fixes anything. What matters is letting the attractors go. Sleep Magic to the rescue!

Assignments for the Recognition Area of Your Life

The following assignment is designed to enhance the recognition that you have for your body since enhancing that will improve your recognition of who you are:

As I am reading this, I allow myself to feel gratitude for all the many ways you help to keep us comfortable and functional.

I notice how you, my wonderful body, are feeling, and I give you permission to relax as we read this, allowing the words to sink deeply into the cellular consciousness of our body.

Now I picture myself asleep in bed tonight, knowing and understanding that you, my beloved body, will take over and put these words into action for me as I am sleeping, that I need to do nothing more than finish reading this.

I know that you know that I see you clearly and that I love you just as you are.

I give you permission now, to the degree that you are comfortable, to release any feelings that you may ever have felt from me or anyone else that were anything less than supportive.

Thank you for helping us to be more open to all the recognition that we have in our lives. I honor you for helping me.

Here's an assignment designed to shift your attractors (and thus, the kind of attention you get):

As I am reading this, I allow myself to feel gratitude for all the many ways you help to keep us comfortable and functional.

I notice how you, my wonderful body, are feeling, and I give you permission to relax as we read this, allowing the words to sink deeply into the cellular consciousness of our body.

Now I picture myself asleep in bed tonight, knowing and understanding that you, my beloved body, will take over and put these words into action for me as I am sleeping, that I need to do nothing more than finish reading this.

I know that you know that we've been attracting attention from (here you can be quite specific or very general), attention that we reject as useless to us, and I know that you know what lies behind this.

So I give you permission now, to the degree that you are comfortable, to release whatever may seem right and appropriate to you in order to let go of whatever it is that we are carrying that is drawing that to us.

Thank you for helping me to become the person I know I am.

Of course, the very opposite may be the case, that you lack attention when you desire it. The reason for that, of course, would be exactly the same: old childhood programming. A little twist on the above assignment turns it around nicely:

As I am reading this, I allow myself to feel gratitude for all the many ways you help to keep us comfortable and functional.

I notice how you, my wonderful body, are feeling, and I give you permission to relax as we read this, allowing the words to sink deeply into the cellular consciousness of our body.

Now I picture myself asleep in bed tonight, knowing and understanding that you, my beloved body, will take over and put these words into action for me as I am sleeping, that I need to do nothing more than finish reading this.

I know that you know that we're not getting the kind of attention that we'd like (or as much attention as we'd like) and I know that you know what lies behind this.

So I give you permission now, to the degree that you are comfortable, to release whatever may seem right and appropriate to you in order to let go of anything that may be keeping us from the recognition we desire.

Thank you for helping me to become the person I know I am.

Not wanting something that you have is energetically very different from wanting something that you don't have. Not wanting something that you have creates a very physical discomfort, much like carrying a ten-pound rock around with you; wanting something that you don't have, though, is usually more of a mental thing and often, the Ego Process can be involved, so care must be taken about being too specific when shifting the vibration toward bringing something to you. That is why, in the second assignment, there is no opportunity for you to be specific. When the only information you can rely on is what your mind is telling you, you have to trust your body to know what is right for you both. Your body will always be your very best advisor.

Because of the Law of Attraction, we are all reflections of each other ... not entirely, but partially. It is as if we were all diamonds and we end up facet to facet with someone who perfectly reflects some aspect of ourselves. In other words, we recognize and are recognized differently all the time. By changing your vibration, you will be recognized differently; you will also see others differently.

If you would like to be recognized for all the kindness or compassion or wisdom that you carry, you need only use Sleep Magic to begin recreating yourself as that person for once you are that person, it will radiate from your being. Humans are, by nature, peaceable and cooperative beings. If that were not the case we would not have survived as a species. I mention this because if what you desire to be seen as is not what comes naturally—is not a primary human trait— then Sleep Magic will simply not work as the body will not recognize your request as basic to its—and your—survival.

So, for example, if you have a desire to be seen as "a leader" you will have to address that by addressing all of the many very human characteristics of being an appropriate leader, one at a time … in other words, you will have to *be* a leader to be seen as one.

You can use this example as a base for your own recreation of yourself:

As I am reading this, I allow myself to feel gratitude to you, my wonderful body, for everything you do for me every day, breathing, circulating my blood and lymph, allowing the food I eat to nourish me, protecting me.

I notice how my body is feeling right now.

Now I picture myself asleep in bed tonight, knowing and understanding that you, my beloved body, will take over and put these words into action for me as I am sleeping, that I need to do nothing more than finish reading this.

I know that you know that I am generally compassionate but I know too that I am sometimes judgmental of others … and myself, so, to the degree that it is possible for you, I give you permission to release whatever lies behind our tendencies to judgment in order to expand our ability to be compassionate.

Thank you, dear body, for helping us to become the person we came here to be.

We've talked a lot about the mind in relation to doing Sleep Magic; most of it has been cautionary information and that will probably always remain the case simply because the mind is not about feelings. Yes, the mind can identify feelings, and that is useful, but it tends to not stop with identifying. That process will walk you down the path of the Ego Process, which needs to know not just what, but why, and begins extrapolating as it attempts to answer all its questions, and you soon find yourself on another path, far from the feeling path, going some other place.

Here's a dramatic and personal example of the mind at work: I'm in a position where it's useful for me to get interviews so that more people can learn about the ease and effectiveness of Sleep Magic and my mind can be very useful in sorting out a good opportunity from a not-so-good opportunity. One evening I received an e-mailed invitation to do an interview for an online radio show. When I first got the invitation my body was tickled; I could tell because my immediate response was, "yes!" But my ever-so-helpful mind piped up and cautioned me to check out the show a little more because the format seemed somewhat confrontational and "I" don't like confrontation, which is to say that my Ego Process would rather avoid it, often at any cost ... but I didn't take my mind's advice. I followed my body's lead instead, my gut response, my first impulse, and I answered yes without checking out another thing. I then I signed off and went to bed.

I did not, however, go to sleep. I couldn't. My mind was revolving, playing out ugly scenario after ugly scenario after ugly scenario, each worse than the last. The Energizer bunny has nothing on my very active mind! Ultimately, after perhaps ninety minutes of this nonsense, I silenced my mind by promising that I would check everything out in the morning and cancel the interview if it was appropriate. I then fell asleep and was awakened about six hours later out of an absolutely hideous nightmare in which I had been behaving very badly, gotten caught in the act, and was about to be publicly humiliated and jailed. Talk about fear!

As I'd lain in bed after waking, still in hypnopompic trance, I'd noticed that I was smiling. Smiling, of all things! After a dream like that. As I was still in that state between sleeping and waking, my mind had yet to kick in, my body had the upper hand and it was smiling. It was smiling because it was happy, because not only had it used the experience as a jumping-off spot for its own healing agenda (and all bodies, except those that are actively engaged in the process of dying, want to be healthy), but it had also provided me with some clarity, illustrating for me exactly how much guilt—and fear of being found out—I was walking around with. That morning smile is vivid proof of why Sleep Magic is done asleep! The mind goes to sleep along with you leaving the body to its work.

After bringing myself back to center I went online to check out the show. It was bright and funny and somewhat irreverent. It was just like me! It was perfect. My mind, at some deep level, was still harboring the guilt of a dissolute youth even now, after almost a decade of doing Sleep Magic, and despite all the amazing and wonderful changes in my life. I'd never even considered that possibility before. I'd been so busy allowing my body to let go of the ramifications of me being a "victim" that I'd neglected my later years of behaving really badly! My body knew where my mind was coming from and it meant to let go because that kind of energy—the kind that makes nightmares—doesn't serve anyone. Its passing brought with it an atmosphere like the one that follows a huge storm, leaving everything feeling preternaturally clear.

My mind has never denied my misspent decades; I've spoken of it openly and often. But neither had I ever utilized Sleep Magic to address all the possible emotional states that I must have been going through at the time. So my Ego Process was still toting around all that guilt thought that I needed to be protected from "protecting." I didn't. But/And that's exactly the sort of thing I'm referring to when I use the phrase "old and outdated programming." In this case the information was old and outdated and really unnecessary ... except as a clue to where I could use Sleep Magic to take me next because there's always better to get!

Trusting Your Inner Knowing

As I am reading this, I allow myself to feel gratitude for everything that you, my beloved body, have done for me today.

I notice how we are feeling, right now, in this moment.

Now I picture myself asleep in bed tonight, knowing and understanding that you, my beloved body, will take over and put these words into action for me as I am sleeping, that I need to do nothing more than finish reading this.

I know that you know that I have a strong sense of what is correct. But I know that you know, too, that sometimes doubt can creep into my thought process, something that is rarely helpful.

So tonight, I ask that you release whatever seems prudent and comfortable to release, in order to allow us to reduce or release doubts when our internal knowingness is secure and correct, thereby allowing our confidence to expand.

I honor you for helping me to be wise and to live in the now.

Untapped Gifts and Potential

As I am reading this, I allow myself to feel gratitude to you, my wonderful body, for everything you do for me every day, breathing, circulating my blood and lymph, allowing the food I eat to nourish me, protecting me.

I notice how my body is feeling right now.

Now I picture myself asleep in bed tonight, knowing and understanding that you, my beloved body, will take over and put these

words into action for me as I am sleeping, that I need to do nothing more than finish reading this.

I know that you know that we hold within us gifts that we have not yet realized. To the degree that it is comfortable for you and appropriate for us, I give you permission to release whatever may stand in the way of those gifts ripening, expanding, and becoming more useful to us.

In the morning I will take note of how I feel. Thank you for helping me to be all that I can be!

8
Relationship

Feng Shui

The Relationship area of the bagua is the hands-down winner in the *Why Do You Want a Feng Shui Consultation?* contest. Relationships are the most valuable currency in our lives. Relationships have shaped this world, and they seem to bring more joy and more pain (sunshine and rain!) than any other part of life ... love relationships, particularly.

The Relationship facet of the bagua map, in the area to the far right of the Entry Wall, covers not only relationships but the nature of relationships, the nurturing, the support, and the enjoyment that they can bring. Remember, as with every other aspect of the bagua, the Relationship area is reflecting you. As well it will also reflect every member of a household so make sure to take that into account when decorating/activating the energy in the area. Setting the tone of the Relationship area in the den of a home where children are present requires that the relationship you are addressing/reflecting is that of the family unit. The personal, private relationship between partners is best addressed in the bedroom or other private spaces.

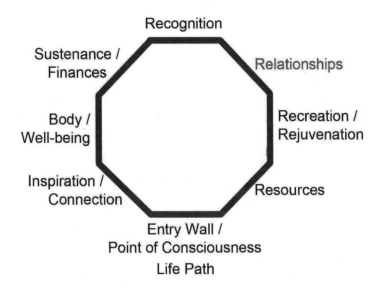

Recognition

Sustenance /
Finances

Relationships

Body /
Well-being

Recreation /
Rejuvenation

Inspiration /
Connection

Resources

Entry Wall /
Point of Consciousness
Life Path

The Relationship area in the bedrooms of young children can include the whole family. Those children younger than seven are still not completely individualized and very much identify with their mothers, fathers, and sometimes siblings, but even older children benefit from feeling as if they are an integral part of a whole. And once hormones kick in, it's especially important to remind older children that they are still part of a family.

For younger children, pictures of them with their parents—either together or separately—are essential, but I prefer to place those images in the Resources area of a child's room, just to the right of his or her headboard (when in the bed), providing a constant influence more felt than seen and one that provides a sense of security while also reminding the child subliminally of the local source of wisdom.

Parental pictures in children's bedrooms are especially important when the parents are not living together ... and provide a good reminder for parents of the necessity of working together for the benefit of the child whose needs trump any differences between the two adults responsible for the existence of said child. The pictures need not be big, just present.

When a child is old enough to request that the pictures of parents be removed from the room then it's likely time to remove them. Don't make a fuss but do appear somewhat saddened, perhaps mentioning, without too much obvious feeling, that, well, you guess they're growing up now, and leave it at that. Ideally, that lets them know that you care that they want to cast you out (energetically), but that you respect their process.

The bedroom of a committed couple is really a Relationship area all its own. Ideally, there's nothing in that room that doesn't relate either to the relationship between the pair or to getting a good night's sleep. Images of paired animals or trees are wonderful but images of the couple are even better. In addition, a man should have on his bureau or near it—preferably on the right, back of the dresser or on the right wall beside it—thus mimicking the position of the Relationship area on the bagua—a photograph—a really good photograph—of his partner.

Much like the images of parents in their children's rooms, this picture is meant to provide a subliminal reminder of the local source of wisdom ... among other things. Men are (generally) more visual creatures than women so the photographs work well to anchor the partner's image in both the conscious and the subconscious mind. I'm not suggesting that men aren't wise, but in the arena of relationships, it's what women biologically excel at.

Why should a man have a picture of his partner by his bureau and a woman not necessarily have one of her partner? Testosterone. It's just that simple. Men and women are biologically different and the drive to reproduce is potent enough to throw some men for a loop so a little extra reminder of where his loyalties lie doesn't hurt.

Important to avoid in the bedroom of a couple are pictures of anyone else. No children, grandchildren, parents, gods, goddesses, or angels. Having pictures of your relatives in the room with you is energetically quite close to actually having them in the room with you. Photographs really can, in some sense, capture your soul ... they certainly make it available for all the world to see at any rate, making the bedroom a tad more crowded—energetically—than is conducive to an intimate relationship.

Sleep Magic

Our first experience of life is the drive to survive. A little body being born is under tremendous pressure—literally—and going through the most remarkable transformation it will ever endure, transitioning from the life of an underwater being to that of a land animal and the first experience it will have out in the world will be in relationship to at least one other human being. Relationship lies at the foundation of what it means to be human. Relationships have created the entire built world and civilization as we know it. Relationships are critical to life on earth.

What we know about relationships begins, as does all our learning, when we are in utero. When a pregnant woman responds, relates, eats, feels, when she does anything, the growing child within her is the recipient of whatever chemical, hormonal cocktail her body dishes up as a result. Our first relationship, with our mother, is completely out of our control but the cells of our bodies, which take all this in, also record and remember the input she—and we—receive so our bodies are born pre-programmed by our mother's responses to the world around her when she was carrying us.

Once we are out in the world we enter into a situation where our relationships will be out of our control for quite a few years, yet our bodies will be absorbing at every moment information about not only the relationships we are experiencing but the relationships that the people around us are having as well, all of this often emotionally laden information becoming a part of who we are, informing us for future use, what relationships are all about.

And so we enter into the years of our development where we begin to feel as if we have some control over things totally unaware that our bodies are running on programming that we, in fact, have very little control over. Our strengths and weakness in the area of relationship become apparent when we reach school-age and social interaction with unknown beings becomes a necessary and practically daily event. We learn how to navigate this world in a hit-or-miss kind of way, figuring out what works ... or not, sitting on the fire escape steps watching our classmates play or being one of the players, not even wondering why that kid over there isn't playing.

Relationship may be the most challenging game of all, and we're all playing all the time, even if we don't want to be, because we have to. The world is built on series of relationships, some so casual that you might not even call them relationships, but they are. The check-out clerk at the store, the teller in the drive-through window, the person who calls you from the doctor's office to remind you of your appointment, you have a relationship with all those people, and they with you. And, fleeting though your contact may be with them, the energy around the interactions colors your day because it's all about energy ... remember?

In a household, the energy of the residents singly and the energy of the residents interacting with each other affects the Feng Shui of the space. Colloquial advice about no arguments at the dinner table and never going to bed angry address that energy because it *doesn't* just go away, it gets absorbed; it gets absorbed by the inanimate furnishings of the space (soft pieces like mattresses and sofas soak up energy as if they were sponges), by the living creatures, and by the people in the space. Children under the age of four are especially vulnerable to this energy as they are still in the time of life when their brains are manufacturing neural connections at a tremendous rate, taking in energetic information as quickly as it is available and helping the cells of the body to form opinions about life ... and relationships; because relationships are, after all, the biggest, most important part of a child's life.

If you struggle with relationships of any kind (and are not suffering from a neural disorder of some sort), be those relationships work related, casual, or intimate, the chances are good that unbeknown to you, the cells of your body are holding onto—and probably carefully guarding—information that is causing that struggle. This is exactly the sort of thing that Sleep Magic can help you to remedy.

For starters (please choose the appropriate gender):

On Being the Man You Are

As I am reading this, I allow myself to feel gratitude to you, my body, for all that you have done for me throughout the course of this day.

I notice how you are feeling, and I give you permission to relax as we are reading this, allowing the words to sink deeply into the cellular consciousness of our body.

Now I picture myself asleep in bed tonight, knowing and understanding that you, my beloved body, will take over and put these words into action for me as I am sleeping, that I need to do nothing more than finish reading this.

I know that we carry within our cells a kind of a map for how a man is "supposed" to be in the world, a map that is based on the men who had the most influence on my life before I was seven years old. There is every chance that a fair amount of this information has nothing to do with how I was designed to be a man in the world. So, since you are well aware of the man that I am, you have my permission tonight to let go—to the degree that you are comfortable—of any old programming that would have me behaving in the world like anyone other than who I truly am at my core.

You can fill the empty space its leaving creates by expanding those aspects of us that are right and true and appropriate to who we came to earth to be.

Thank you for helping me to feel more truly all that I am.

On Being the Woman That You Are

As I am reading this, I allow myself to feel gratitude to you, my body, for all that you have done for me throughout the course of this day.

I notice how you are feeling, and I give you permission to relax as we are reading this, allowing the words to sink deeply into the cellular consciousness of our body.

Now I picture myself asleep in bed tonight, knowing and understanding that you, my beloved body, will take over and put these words into action for me as I am sleeping, that I need to do nothing more than finish reading this.

I know that we carry within our cells a kind of a map for how a woman is "supposed" to be in the world, a map that is based on the women who had the most influence on my life before I was seven years old. There is every chance that a fair amount of this information has nothing to do with the way that I have been designed to be a woman in the world. So, since you are well aware of the woman that I am, you have my permission tonight to let go—to the degree that you are comfortable—of any old programming that would have me behaving in the world like anyone other than who I truly am at my core.

You can fill the empty space its leaving creates by expanding those aspects of us that are right and true and appropriate to who we came to earth to be.

Thank you for helping me to be more truly all that I am.

On Attracting a Partner

If intimate relationships have proved challenging for you and you'd like to address that, then you might want to use Sleep Magic to assist you in letting go of whatever is hiding inside you, causing that problem. The following assignment could prove useful and, as with other deeply entrenched issues, may require repetition every seven to ten days or so.

As I am reading this, I allow myself to feel gratitude to you, my wonderful body, for everything you do for me every day, breathing, circulating my blood and lymph, allowing the food I eat to nourish me, protecting me.

I notice how my body is feeling right now.

Now I picture myself asleep in bed tonight, knowing and understanding that you, my beloved body, will take over and put these words into action for me as I am sleeping, that I need to do nothing more than finish reading this.

I know that you know that there is, out there in the world, a perfect partner for me.

So, to the degree that it is comfortable for you, I give you permission to release whatever might stand in the way of my attracting that partner.

You can fill the empty space the leaving energies create by expanding the feeling I have when I am really happy with myself (for whatever reason).

I honor you for helping me.

Have you ever done that sort of list-making thing where you piece together the qualities of the partner of your dreams? Even if you have, it might be time to do it again adding Sleep Magic to the process.

To begin, make a list of the qualities you have to offer a partner.

On the first two nights, check with your body to see how it feels about those lists because it is possible that some of what you *think* you want is based on childhood programming that is not appropriate to the grown-up person that you have become. It is also possible that your list about yourself is not entirely accurate; you may have missed things or incorrectly evaluated yourself. Your body will let you know by either bringing you feelings in dream that are clues or by bringing you an immediate waking awareness.

By taking the elements of your lists into sleep for your body to consider, and perhaps comment on, you present your body with the opportunity to remind you of things you may have forgotten, overlooked, or simply be entirely wrong about.

If any of the dreams you have—or the way you feel when you awaken—is anything outside of the range of neutral to good, then you may have some work to do before you proceed to the next two steps of the process. Use the standard "follow-up" assignment to let your body know that you are aware that something is amiss and give it permission to let go of whatever may be causing the glitch (to the degree that it is comfortable in so doing, of course) or to bring the matter to the attention of your waking conscious mind for further consideration. You can then give it permission to expand whatever it feels would be appropriate if it needs to fill any empty energetic space.

You'll need two nights for each list, four nights total. The first two nights, we've just dealt with. Once that is done, and everything set right if it needed to be, you can proceed to the third night on which you will tell your Body Intelligence that you know it remembers the list you made about yourself, giving it permission to release whatever it may need to in order to enhance your good qualities.

On the fourth night you can address releasing that which would allow you to more easily attract the partner you desire and let your body know that it has your permission to expand whatever it would find appropriate to fill any empty energetic space that may be created.

If anyone has ever questioned your ability to commit—even if you didn't agree with them—the following assignment might be worth doing. After all, you know what you know ... but you don't know what you don't know!

Avoiding Relationships

As I am reading this, I allow myself to feel gratitude for everything that you do for me throughout the days, for nourishing me and sustaining me, for keeping me safe and strong.

I notice how you, body, are feeling, and I give you permission to relax as we read these words, allowing them to sink deep into our body consciousness.

Now I picture myself asleep in bed tonight, knowing and understanding that you, my beloved body, will take over and put these words into action for me as I am sleeping, that I need to do nothing more than finish reading this.

Dear body, I know that you know that my general tendency is to avoid even the subject of intimate relationship, and I know that you, better than anyone else, would know what lies behind that choice, a choice that I am sure has been serving some purpose.

In the interest of being all that we can be at this time, I want to give you permission, to the degree that you are comfortable, to release as much of whatever it was that originally caused that tendency as you can.

You can fill the empty space its leaving creates by gently expanding the genuine good feelings that I have about myself as a person.

Thank you for helping me to become more comfortable in life.

Feeling Vulnerable

Sometimes, a feeling that we could be open to being hurt stands in the way of entering into and/or committing to an intimate relationship. Such a feeling may have been generated by any number of circumstances. The following assignment is a good place to start the exploration.

Thank you, dear body, for all the work you did for me today. I am so grateful for breathing and for my blood circulating, for digesting food and casting off what we do not need.

I notice how my body is feeling right now, as I read this.

Now I picture myself asleep in bed tonight, knowing and understanding that you, my beloved body, will take over and put these words into action for me as I am sleeping, that I need to do nothing more than finish reading this.

I know that you know that I am shaking in my boots over the feelings that _____ is stirring up in me. I know, too, that it is really pretty silly and disturbing to have this going on so I give you permission, to the degree that you are comfortable, to let go of whatever is behind this resistance to feeling vulnerable.

You can fill the empty space its leaving creates by expanding the way I felt/feel _____. (A time when you took a risk, went out on a limb, and it worked! You felt great.)

Thank you for helping me to live deeply and well. I love you!

Attracting a Suitable Match

As I am reading this, I allow myself to feel gratitude to you, my wonderful body, for everything you do for me every day, breathing, circulating my blood and lymph, allowing the food I eat to nourish me, protecting me.

I notice how my body is feeling right now.

Now I picture myself asleep in bed tonight, knowing and under-standing that you, my beloved body, will take over and put these words into action for me as I am sleeping, that I need to do nothing more than finish reading this.

I know that you know that there is, out there in the world, some-one who can match my intelligence, character, and tendencies and who would make a great companion for me.

So, to the degree that it is comfortable for you, I give you per-mission to release whatever seems right and appropriate, that our attraction for such a person may shine ever more brightly.

Thank you for helping me to be the most content, fulfilled, and satisfied that I can be.

Attracting the "Perfect Partner"

As I am reading this, I allow myself to feel gratitude to you, my wonderful body, for everything you do for me every day, breathing, circulating my blood and lymph, allowing the food I eat to nourish me, protecting me.

I notice how my body is feeling right now.

Now I picture myself asleep in bed tonight, knowing and under-standing that you, my beloved body, will take over and put these words into action for me as I am sleeping, that I need to do nothing more than finish reading this.

I know that you know that there is, out there in the world, a perfect partner for me.

So, to the degree that it is comfortable for you, I give you per-mission to release whatever might stand in the way of my attracting that partner.

You can fill the empty space the leaving energies create by ex-panding the feeling I have when I am really, really good with who I am.

In the morning when I awaken I will take note of how I feel. I honor you for helping me.

Worthy of Love—Expanding

As I am reading this, dear body, I allow myself to feel gratitude for everything that you do for me throughout the days, for nourishing me and sustaining me, for keeping me safe and strong.

I notice how you, body, are feeling, and I give you permission to relax as we read these words, allowing them to sink deep into our body consciousness.

Now I picture myself asleep in bed tonight, knowing and understanding that you, my beloved body, will take over and put these words into action for me as I am sleeping, that I need to do nothing more than finish reading this.

Dear body, I suspect that there is some chance that somewhere deep inside us I do not feel worthy of love. That feeling does not serve us and, in addition to that, is simply a lie. So I give you permission to release that feeling and whatever it was that caused it.

You can fill the empty space its leaving creates by expanding, with as much passion as you feel comfortable with, the intellectual knowing I have that I am, in fact, worthy of love.

In the morning when I awaken I will take note of how I feel. Thank you!

Feeling Lovable

As I am reading this, dear body, I allow myself to feel gratitude (for something, anything).

I notice how you, body, are feeling.

Now I picture myself asleep in bed tonight, knowing and understanding that you, my beloved body, will take over and put these words into action for me as I am sleeping, that I need to do nothing more than finish reading this.

Intellectually I know that you and I deserve to be loved and I have a sense that you know this with even more surety than I do, at a cellular and spiritual level, so, to the degree that it is comfortable for you, I give you permission to release whatever might stand in the way of my expanding and fully embracing the totality of my lovability.

In the morning when I awaken I will take note of how I feel. Thank you!

Being Able to Be Loved

As I am reading this, I allow myself to feel gratitude to you, my wonderful body, for everything you do for me every day, breathing, circulating my blood and lymph, allowing the food I eat to nourish me, protecting me.

I notice how you are feeling right now, and I give you permission as you read these words to relax, allowing the words to sink deep into our cellular consciousness.

Now I picture myself asleep in bed tonight, knowing and understanding that you, my beloved body, will take over and put these words into action for me as I am sleeping, that I need to do nothing more than finish reading this.

I know that you remember that feeling, from when we were very, very small, of being loved unconditionally. To the degree that it is comfortable for you, I give you permission to release whatever you might need to in order to allow that feeling to become more a part of who we are.

In the morning when I awaken I will take note of how I feel. I honor you for helping me.

Releasing a Tendency to Attract Unsuitable Partners

As I am reading this, dear body, I allow myself to feel gratitude for all the many ways you help to keep us comfortable and functional.

I notice how you, my wonderful body, are feeling, and I give you permission to relax as we read this, allowing the words to sink deeply into the cellular consciousness of our body.

Now I picture myself asleep in bed tonight, knowing and understanding that you, my beloved body, will take over and put these words into action for me as I am sleeping, that I need to do nothing more than finish reading this.

I know that you remember our first attraction to _____. I've changed a lot since then, and I'd like to ask you to help me to change even more by releasing whatever was behind my choosing a partner who was less than ideal for me.

You can fill any empty space that is created by expanding the energy around how I feel from you when I get the sense that something (anything!) is just perfect for me.

Thank you for helping me to create a life that feels just right!

Releasing the Feelings and Energy of a Failed Attraction

As I am reading this, I allow myself to feel gratitude for all the many ways you help to keep us comfortable and functional.

I notice how you, my wonderful body, are feeling, and I give you permission to relax as we read this, allowing the words to sink deeply into the cellular consciousness of our body.

Now I picture myself asleep in bed tonight, knowing and understanding that you, my beloved body, will take over and put these words into action for me as I am sleeping, that I need to do nothing more than finish reading this.

I know that you remember our attraction to _____, an attraction that I still feel, now with some (pain/heartbreak/guilt/whatever) attached. This current condition is less than useful to me and I wish to let it go, so to the degree that you are comfortable, I give you permission to release it.

You can fill any empty space that is created by expanding the love that I feel for myself and for you.

Thank you for helping me to create a life that works for me!

This assignment could easily be modified to fit almost any lingering and unwanted feelings. It is one of the few times that one is not releasing what is behind something because, presumably, you have already addressed that previously, allowing your body to let go of whatever drew such a situation to you in the first place.

Parental Model for Relationship—Releasing

As I am reading this, I allow myself to feel gratitude for everything that you do for me throughout the days, for nourishing me and sustaining me, for keeping me safe and strong.

I notice how you, body, are feeling, and I give you permission to relax as we read these words, allowing them to sink deep into our body consciousness.

Now I picture myself asleep in bed tonight, knowing and understanding that you, my beloved body, will take over and put these words into action for me as I am sleeping, that I need to do nothing more than finish reading this.

Dear body, I know that we are carrying around a model for action—programming—that we received from our parents as to what a relationship between a man and a woman looks like ... and it looks pretty poor. So to the degree that it is comfortable and possible for you, I give you permission to let go of that model.

You can fill the empty space its leaving creates by expanding the way I felt/feel when _____. (A time when you felt balanced and peaceful performing a task or doing an activity of some sort.)

In the morning when I awaken I will take note of how I feel. Thank you!

Childhood Decisions about Relationships—Step-Siblings

The relationships we have with siblings color our childhood—and our expectations about relationships—tremendously. When those siblings have been "imported" into a household already grown, the normal range of sibling rivalries and challenges is made even more complex, and it can show up in adult life as an underlying current that makes intimate relationships seem more daunting.

As I am reading this, I allow myself to feel gratitude to you, my wonderful body, for everything you do for me every day, breathing, circulating my blood and lymph, allowing the food I eat to nourish me, protecting me.

I notice how you, my body, are feeling right now, and I give you permission to relax as we read this.

Now I picture myself asleep in bed tonight, knowing and understanding that you, my beloved body, will take over and put these words into action for me as I am sleeping, that I need to do nothing more than finish reading this.

I know that you remember how we felt when our step-siblings became a part of our family, and I know too that the introduction of "outsiders" into what had been a known and comfortable environment was disturbing to our sense of what we could count on in life.

If I made any decisions about avoiding relationships because I was carrying insecurity about that time in my life, I give you permission to let go of them, to the degree that you are comfortable doing so.

You can fill the empty space their leaving creates by expanding the intellectual knowingness I have that I have a say in any relationships I may enter into at this point in my life.

I honor you for helping me to feel more confident in my world.

Suitability of Someone as a Life Partner

Thank you, dear body, for all the work you did for me today. I am so grateful for breathing and for my blood circulating, for digesting food and casting off what we do not need.

As I read this I allow myself to become aware of my breath, of how my muscles are feeling, if I feel limited anywhere in our body or if I feel any pain or discomfort.

Now, I imagine myself getting into bed tonight, getting as comfortable as I can be, feeling myself beginning to relax, knowing that you, my wonderfully hard-working body, will be processing this request for us as we sleep.

I know that you have been and are carrying around a lot of conflicting feelings about our relationship to ____, as a life partner. I need clarity on this subject, and I know that you have it, so, to the degree that you are comfortable, I give you permission to release whatever you may need to in order to expand that clarity.

Thank you for hearing me and for working with me in our behalf. I promise to listen to what you tell me. I love you.

Avoiding Conflict by Withholding Information

As I am reading this, I allow myself to feel gratitude to you, my wonderful body, for everything you do for me every day, breathing, circulating my blood and lymph, allowing the food I eat to nourish me, protecting me.

I notice how you are feeling right now and give you permission to relax as we read this, allowing the words to deeply penetrate our cellular consciousness.

Now I picture myself asleep in bed tonight, knowing and understanding that you, my beloved body, will take over and put these words into action for me as I am sleeping, that I need to do nothing more than finish reading this.

I know that you know that, in an attempt to soften a blow, I will sometimes hold back on information that I want to communicate, waiting for "a better time" to say what I really want to say. I know that you know, too, that sometimes that "better time" never comes.

You know what is behind this tendency to delay and withhold, and you know too that it doesn't really serve any of the parties involved so to the degree that it is comfortable for you, I give you permission to release whatever lies behind this.

You can fill the empty space that is created by expanding the feeling of relief I experienced when _____. (A time when you got something off your chest and it felt good.)

Thank you for helping me to be everything I came here to be. I love you!

Sleep Magic has been designed to clear the way for you to be everything you can be. In doing that, it is changing your vibration. And because we are creatures of vibrational attraction, you may find that your relationships are changing as well. We have attracted people to ourselves based on how our vibrations resonated when we met, if either party changes vibration along the way, the whole dynamic of the relationship can change.

Be aware. You may find new people coming into your life and some old people slipping away. That may be disconcerting, but remember this, if you hold onto those vibrations that are no longer really "you" because the people who carry them are familiar and you have grown fond of them, you will be nourishing some part of you that you are, through Sleep Magic, also trying to change. That is a difficult balancing act.

Now, it happens that when someone really close to you senses your vibration changing, they *can* begin to change as well, trying to keep up with you. If you really like them, look for opportunities to assist them as they strive to move forward. Nothing obvious, nothing blatant, but just look for subtle changes as they may, perhaps, do something a little differently than they did before, or say something you would not have expected. If you want to keep their friendship and their love, respond to them in a slightly different way than you might have before, allowing them some room to grow ... or leave if they must.

We tend to develop patterns of behavior and modes of response in any relationship. Sometimes those are fun and bonding, other times they are limiting, locking you into an old mode of behavior that will keep you from becoming all that you are. Be aware of what serves your growth as a person and be aware of how your change can pave the way for another's change. Growing wise together is a wonderful thing.

FAMILY

Most of us are used to taking other people into account when we make decisions about our lives, and that's an admirable thing if the other people in question can be affected by your actions in a way that would be deleterious to them. But if you have your heart set on a bright yellow sofa and your sister reminds you pointedly that a bright yellow sofa would simply horrify your mother, then we are not talking about life and death. We are talking about the difference between you having something in your life that will lift your spirits every time you see it or you irritating your mother. Your furniture and your happiness is your business. Grown-up people know that. Good parents allow for it. If your mother's irritation with your choice of a sofa is going to affect your life in a profound way, then your relationship with your mother could use some adjusting ... in your head ... and possibly—probably!—in the cellular intelligence of your body. Sleep Magic can help you do that.

FATHER

Father—Absent

I notice how my body is feeling, and I am grateful to it for supporting me in every way.

I picture myself asleep in bed tonight, knowing and understanding that you, my beloved body, will take over and put these words into action for me as I am sleeping, that I need to do nothing more than finish reading this.

I know that you know that when we were young our father was not around much. I know, too, that it is possible that I may have felt as though I were less important to him than the things that kept him away. If indeed you are holding onto any feelings like that, I give you permission, to the degree that you are comfortable, to let them go.

You can fill the empty space its leaving creates by expanding the energy I had that felt like love one time when my father held me and seemed genuinely happy to be holding me (even though I may not consciously remember that moment, I know that you do).

I thank you for working with me to become everything that I came here to be.

Father—Judgmental

As I am reading this, I allow myself to feel gratitude to you, my wonderful body, for everything you do for me every day, breathing, circulating my blood and lymph, allowing the food I eat to nourish me, protecting me.

I notice how my body is feeling right now.

Now I picture myself asleep in bed tonight, knowing and understanding that you, my beloved body, will take over and put these words into action for me as I am sleeping, that I need to do nothing more than finish reading this.

I know that you know how judgmental our father was. If I am carrying with me any harsh judgments he made about me, I give you permission to release them to the degree that you are comfortable in doing so.

I give you permission to fill any empty space that may be created by expanding the love I feel/felt _____.

In the morning when I awaken I will take note of how I feel. I honor you for helping me.

Father—Not Living Up to (Imagined or Expressed) Expectations

As I am reading this, I allow myself to feel gratitude to you, my wonderful body, for everything you do for me every day, breathing, circulating my blood and lymph, allowing the food I eat to nourish me, protecting me.

I notice how my body is feeling right now, and I give you permission to relax as we are reading these words.

Now I picture myself asleep in bed tonight, knowing and understanding that you, my beloved body, will take over and put these words into action for me as I am sleeping, that I need to do nothing more than finish reading this.

I know that you know how much our father meant to us when we were young. If I may have compared myself unfavorably to what I thought were his standards for me, and am still holding onto any of those unfavorable judgments as decisions about who I am, I give you permission to release them to the degree that you are comfortable in doing so.

I give you permission to fill any empty space that may be created by expanding the confidence I have felt in myself _____.

In the morning when I awaken I will take note of how I feel. I honor you for helping me.

Father—Disliked Qualities

As I am reading this, I allow myself to feel gratitude to you, my wonderful body, for everything you do for me every day, breathing, circulating my blood and lymph, allowing the food I eat to nourish me, protecting me.

I notice how my body is feeling right now.

Now I picture myself asleep in bed tonight, knowing and understanding that you, my beloved body, will take over and put these words into action for me as I am sleeping, that I need to do nothing more than finish reading this.

I know that you know that my father has many qualities that I do not like. I know, too, that many of those qualities exist in me at least to some degree. To the degree that it is comfortable for you, I give you permission to release any judgment we may have carried about those qualities.

You can fill the empty space their leaving creates by expanding the feeling of compassion that I can now have for my father.

In the morning when I awaken I will take note of how I feel.

Thank you for assisting me in becoming comfortable in and with the life we are living.

Releasing Father's Negative Projections

As I am reading this, I allow myself to feel gratitude to you, my wonderful body, for everything you do for me every day, breathing, circulating my blood and lymph, allowing the food I eat to nourish me, protecting me.

I notice how my body is feeling right now.

Now I picture myself asleep in bed tonight, knowing and understanding that you, my beloved body, will take over and put these words into action for me as I am sleeping, that I need to do nothing more than finish reading this.

I know that you know how much our father meant to us when we were young. If I may have absorbed from him any doubt about my having a wonderful life and am still holding onto any of that doubt as decisions about who I am, and what I can have in the world, I give you permission to release it to the degree that you are comfortable in doing so.

I give you permission to fill any empty space that may be created by expanding the confidence I have felt in myself _____.

In the morning when I awaken I will take note of how I feel. I honor you for helping me.

MOTHER

Mother—Not Living Up to (Imagined or Expressed) Expectations

As I am reading this, I allow myself to feel gratitude to you, my wonderful body, for everything you do for me every day, breathing, circulating my blood and lymph, allowing the food I eat to nourish me, protecting me.

I notice how you, my body, are feeling right now, and I give you permission to relax as we read this note.

Now I picture myself asleep in bed tonight, knowing and understanding that you, my beloved body, will take over and put these words into action for me as I am sleeping, that I need to do nothing more than finish reading this.

I know that you know how much our mother meant to us when we were young. If I may have compared myself unfavorably to what I thought were her standards for me, and am still holding onto any of those unfavorable judgments as decisions about who I am, I give you permission to release them to the degree that you are comfortable in doing so.

I give you permission to fill any empty space that may be created by expanding the confidence I have felt in myself _____.

Thank you for helping me to be more comfortable with who I am.

Releasing Mother's Negative Projections

As I am reading this, I allow myself to feel gratitude to you, my wonderful body, for everything you do for me every day, breathing, circulating my blood and lymph, allowing the food I eat to nourish me, protecting me.

I notice how my body is feeling right now.

Now I picture myself asleep in bed tonight, knowing and understanding that you, my beloved body, will take over and put these words into action for me as I am sleeping, that I need to do nothing more than finish reading this.

I know that you know how much our mother meant to us when we were young. If I may have absorbed from her any doubt about my having a wonderful life and am still holding onto any of that doubt as decisions about who I am, and what I can have in the world, I give you permission to release it to the degree that you are comfortable in doing so.

I give you permission to fill any empty space that may be created by expanding the confidence I have felt in myself _____.

In the morning when I awaken I will take note of how I feel. I honor you for helping me.

Mother—Disliked Qualities

As I am reading this, I allow myself to feel gratitude to you, my wonderful body, for everything you do for me every day, breathing, circulating my blood and lymph, allowing the food I eat to nourish me, protecting me.

I notice how my body is feeling right now.

Now I picture myself asleep in bed tonight, knowing and understanding that you, my beloved body, will take over and put these words into action for me as I am sleeping, that I need to do nothing more than finish reading this.

I know that you know that my mother has many qualities that I do not like. I know, too, that many of those qualities exist in me at least to some degree. To the degree that it is comfortable for you, I give you permission to release any judgment we may have carried about those qualities.

You can fill the empty space their leaving creates by expanding the feeling of compassion that I can now have for my mother.

In the morning when I awaken I will take note of how I feel.

Thank you for assisting me in becoming comfortable in and with the life we are living.

PARENTS

ARGUING—Feeling Helpless

As I am reading this, my dear body, I allow myself to feel gratitude for everything you have done in my behalf today, for breathing, for digesting, incorporating, and eliminating, for protecting us from harm, for all that you do.

I notice how you and I are feeling right now, and I give you permission to relax a little if you feel so inclined.

Now I picture myself asleep in bed tonight.

I know that you remember how our parents used to argue and how helpless that made me feel. There was nothing I could do, no place to which I could escape. That feeling of helplessness has no place in my life and is not serving me well so I give you permission, to the degree that you are comfortable, to release it.

You can fill the empty space their leaving may create by expanding the way I feel when _____. (I'm definitely "in charge.")

I honor you for helping me to feel strong and confident in the world.

ARGUING—Feeling Scared

As I am reading this, dear body, I allow myself to feel gratitude for everything you have done in my behalf today, for breathing, for digesting, incorporating, and eliminating, for protecting us from harm, for all that you do.

I notice how you and I are feeling right now, and I give you permission to relax a little if you feel so inclined.

Now I picture myself asleep in bed tonight.

I know that you remember how our parents used to argue and how scared that made me feel. That feeling of being scared has no place in my life and is not serving me well so I give you permission, to the degree that you are comfortable, to release it.

You can fill the empty space their leaving may create by expanding the way I feel when _____. (Expand a feeling of safety or security that you have when engaged in a particular act or situation, like snuggled in bed.)

In the morning when I awaken I will take note of how I feel. I honor you for helping me to be all that I can be.

ARGUING—Feeling Responsible

Sometimes parents argue about their children because they disagree on child-rearing techniques. But any young child, overhearing such an argument, hearing his or her name mentioned in the heat of it, may feel as though the argument would not have happened had it not been for their actions ... and of course, it wouldn't have, so the logic is almost flawless, making it very believable to the child in question that the disagreement is his or her fault.

As I am reading this, I allow myself to feel gratitude for everything you, my dear body, have done in my behalf today, for breathing, for digesting, incorporating, and eliminating, for protecting us from harm, for all that you do.

I notice how you and I are feeling right now, and I give you permission to relax a little if you feel so inclined.

Now I picture myself asleep in bed tonight.

I know that you remember how our parents used to argue and sometimes that arguing might have been about something concerning me. Knowing who I am I know that I might have felt responsible, to some degree, for their disagreement. That feeling of responsibility is misplaced and less than useful to me so I give you permission, to the degree that you are comfortable, to release it.

You can fill the empty space their leaving may create by expanding whatever feels right and appropriate to you.

In the morning when I awaken I will take note of how I feel. I honor you for helping me to be all that I can be.

HOARDING

As I am reading this, dear body, I allow myself to feel gratitude for everything you have done in my behalf today, for breathing, for digesting, incorporating, and eliminating, for protecting us from harm, for all that you do.

I notice how you and I are feeling right now, and I give you permission to relax a little if you feel so inclined.

Now I picture myself asleep in bed tonight.

I know that you remember how our (father/mother) tended to hoard things, and I know that you know why he/she did that. Whatever (his/her/their reasons), any tendency toward hoarding would be detrimental to me in the life I am creating for myself, so if I absorbed any of (his/her/their) reasons for hoarding, I give you permission, to the degree that you are comfortable, to release them.

You can fill the empty space their leaving may create by expanding the way I feel when I reorganize and/or tidy up my personal spaces.

In the morning when I awaken I will take note of how I feel. I honor you for helping me to be all that I can be.

FRIENDS

Holding Grudges

As I am reading this, my dear body, I allow myself to feel gratitude for everything that you do for me throughout the days, for nourishing me and sustaining me, for keeping me safe and strong.

I notice how you, body, are feeling, and I give you permission to relax as we read these words, allowing them to sink deep into our body consciousness.

Now I picture myself asleep in bed tonight, knowing and understanding that you, my beloved Body, will take over and put these words into action for me as I am sleeping, that I need to do nothing more than finish reading this.

Dear body, I know that you know that I tend to hold grudges against those who have made me feel badly. And you know better than I do that holding grudges is a waste of energy and even takes away from your sense of well-being. You know, too, why I do this; you know what's behind it and, since it doesn't really do either of us any good, I give you permission, to the degree that you are comfortable doing to let go of whatever has caused this tendency.

You can fill the empty space its leaving creates by expanding the way I felt/feel when _____. (... you "made up" after a disagreement with someone and felt good about it. If such a thing never occurred, simply give your body permission to expand whatever feels correct for it to do.)

Thank you for helping us both to be comfortable and healthy!

Attracting Friends (or a Partner)

Thank you, my beloved body, for all that you have done for me over the course of the last day. I notice how you are feeling at this moment, and I give you permission to relax as we read this, allowing these words to enter easily into our consciousness.

(If not actually in bed) I imagine us resting in bed, our mind slowly letting go of the activities of the day that have occupied it.

I know that you know that I have difficulty attracting (friends/a partner) and I know that you know, too, why this is. It would feel good to me to have such a person in my life and so, if there is anything that you could release for me, from our great bank of cellular information, I would very much appreciate it.

If doing so would make you feel empty or somehow less than you are, you have my permission to expand the growing love and respect that I feel for you.

Thank you very much for helping me to feel more comfortable in the world.

Recreation and Rejuvenation

Feng Shui

Directly opposite from the Body/Well-being area of the bagua, lies what I call Recreation and Rejuvenation. In the old schools of Feng Shui where each portion of the bagua was identified by a hexagram from the ancient book of divination, the I Ching, this area was marked by the hexagram called Lake. Lake referred to the Lake of the Gods, a mythical place where supernatural beings hung out and kicked back between adventures. It is an area associated with the kind of effortless power that can only be born of experience and applied intelligence, and it implies a confidence that is inherent in the very cells of a being. This is the place where achievement comes to rest itself that it may achieve even more.

In many current schools of Feng Shui this facet of the bagua is associated with vacations and recreational pastimes, but that has always seemed to me to skim the surface of the lake, for the waters here run deep. What is implied in this area, what lies beneath an immediately visible surface, is that an individual has *earned* the right to be in this place. You recreate yourself here through relaxation as a reward for having spent your energy wisely and well. There is a mature energy here, the flow of energy having made its way almost all the way around the octagon. To activate the energy of this area is to make a promise to yourself about your own future.

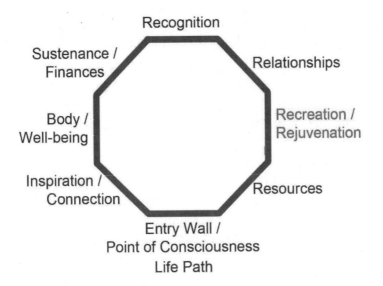

Recognition

Sustenance / Finances

Relationships

Body / Well-being

Recreation / Rejuvenation

Inspiration / Connection

Resources

Entry Wall /
Point of Consciousness
Life Path

In the times of very traditional, old-school Feng Shui, art was a far more literal thing than we know it to be today. And even two decades ago in the United States, most Feng Shui teachers shied away from using abstract works to enliven the energy of a given area of the home, but for me, for this area, an area that speaks, for those in their twenties and thirties, to a time in life that may actually be unimaginable to them, abstract works of art offer something that more literal images cannot; they offer something that is very much in keeping with the energies of the gods that were associated with this area, a space where imagination can play ... and imagination may be the most god-like human attribute there is.

I have brought up numerous times the idea of using metaphorical images to mirror the ways in which you see yourself in the world ... but why limit yourself to what you know where your so-called future is involved? Being goal oriented can be a helpful thing, but to be so focused on something that you close yourself off from options that might keep you from attaining more than you may have thought yourself capable of may not be a helpful thing.

The free play of color in abstract works summons up feelings from the body. This is not a baseless statement; there are entire books written about the effect of color on the human body, Faber-Birren's being among the most respected.

What colors make you feel happy? Content? Peaceful? How would you like to *feel* as you move into the fullness of your being? What would your future look like in terms of color?

Some abstract artworks create shapes that are filled with references to reality, with faces and bodies and beings that are not "really" there, but which you, from a certain angle, can see. These works stimulate your brain, teasing it to make sense of something that isn't even there ... kind of like life.

My very first Feng Shui teacher, Melinda Joy, whom I chose specifically because her approach was informed by her Native American roots, used to caution her students not to limit their possibilities by making specific statements about what they wanted to have come to them because, after all, they might unintentionally close the door on some even more amazing possibilities that they were simply unable to imagine at that point in their lives. When she wanted something of the Universe she would always leave the door open, "This," she would say, "I'd like this or something better."

See the Relaxation and Rejuvenation area as a place where your imagination can run rampant, without your Ego Process judging the inspirations that bubble up. Think "future" for this segment of your spaces ... and leave the door ajar.

Sleep Magic

This area of the bagua, as it nears the end of its cycling, has a lot to do with the soul. Sometimes people mistake the soul for the spirit and vice versa. I suppose the reasons for that are twofold. First of all, you can't see either of them, and second, very few people address the differences between the two. I'm about to do that.

Imagine the following scenario. It is a hot day, a very hot day, we are on a tropical island just outside a very upscale hotel. A white limousine with dark-tinted windows has just pulled under the large porte cocher where any number of hotel employees, all in their uniforms, are waiting to attend to the passenger of the limousine. The driver exits his door and walks around to the passenger door on the opposite side. He opens the door. One beautifully shaped leg slides into view closely followed by another. The shoes are fabulous, with almost impossibly high heels but they are perfectly balanced as is the handsome woman who emerges to stand on them.

The woman exits the car and makes her way through the door that is being held open for her. Back at the limo, the bell person is busily piling luggage from the trunk to a shiny brass luggage carrier. There are so many suitcases and bags and hanging items that she is forced to carry some of the loose pieces draped over her arm. While the entitled passenger of the private car is signing in at the desk, the bell person is struggling to backside bump her way through the door tugging the overloaded luggage cart behind her while making very, very, very sure not to drop anything.

Just as the bell person approaches the desk, the handsome woman executes a perfect quarter turn and heads down the marble hall to the elevator that will carry her to her room. The bell person, attempting to appear as if this amazing juggling act she is pulling off is absolutely effortless, attempts to keep pace.

That elegant, entitled woman, energetically clicking her $700 heels against the marble floor, is spirit. That bell person, struggling to keep up, trying to hold it all together, is soul.

The spirit is the essence of who you are that exists as a part of all that is. Spirit is the part of you that *is* you as you in the grandest sense of your existence in every dimension in which you exist. Soul exists in the dimensions in which spirit has embodied as a human ... and it's the one carrying all the baggage!

The function of the soul is to carry the emotional information of all the lifetimes. That's what it does. Somebody has to keep track. The soul is the living record of all that you are in every dimension in which you exist as an embodied creature. And that is why, if not properly thanked, the soul can get a little surly. It's a tough job carrying all that baggage around. Even for those of us whose spirits choose to experience life at a fairly easy vibrational pace, it's a tough job because, as humans, we experience loss. No matter how sweet a life we live, it will be touched at some points by loss. The human body dies. We lose the very elements that have made our life sweet. If we are healthy, functioning people, we do what we call, getting over it ... eventually. Sometimes it takes longer than others. But the soul ... the soul can't ever get over it. And the soul is keeping track of those losses for lifetime after lifetime after lifetime ad infinitum.

So if we're smart, we do for the soul what that very elegant woman will do for the bell person, we say thank you like we mean it and we tip well. Many years ago, when I'd been doing hands-on healing for about five years straight, pretty much without a break, I took a week-long class that was very much the equivalent of a modern-day mystery school experience. As part of our journey we experienced a guided meditation, led by our instructor, in which we were to take our soul on vacation. Well, I had a wonderful time. My soul and I went off to a beautiful tropical island, palm trees swaying in a constant yet gentle breeze, waters the color of turquoise and just warm enough to be refreshingly inviting. We were paddling about in shallow waters when we got the call to come back.

I began to move toward shore when I heard, behind me, my soul hollering out, "b'bye."

I stopped dead in the water. "B'bye?" I queried.

"Yeah," it said happily. "See you in about sixteen years."

"Sixteen years?!" And from somewhere outside my reverie I heard the facilitator impressing upon us the need to return to a state of normal consciousness. I looked at my soul; my soul looked back. My soul looked just about as happy as I felt perplexed. I didn't know what to do. I was supposed to go back. It waved as it smiled at me, clearly intent on staying right where it was, and I had pretty much no choice but to swim back to the so-called real world, alone.

Now I didn't come back soul-less, this was a metaphorical vacation, after all, but I got the hint. I scheduled a series of soul-restorative treatments with an old friend who does color puncture; I cut back on my client load; and I took a long overdue vacation. Finally, one day, months and months later, I was able to lure my soul back from its metaphorical rogue vacation.

If your soul is tired, you'll know it ... one way or another. If you are what people have come to characterize as depressed, that's a sure sign that your soul is just plain worn out, and it's one of the reasons why I am opposed to the more or less wholesale distribution of so-called antidepressants. They have their place certainly. Some people need them. But everybody doesn't need them! Some days it seems like every other person I meet is taking some antidepressant or another, but we're supposed to feel sad sometimes ... there's information you need to know about in sadness, there's wisdom in grief, and both are signs that your soul needs attention. While drugs can trick the body into feeling perkier, they don't fool the soul even a little ... and they don't fix what's really wrong.

On the other hand, if you really know how to take care of yourself in a balanced, healthy way, chances are your soul is perfectly content. And, just so you know, balanced and healthy does not necessarily mean that you meditate every day or do yoga. Meditation and yoga are both excellent tools for people who respond well to them but, like any tool, they can be misused and, like any tool, some people respond to them more than others do. If you do what you love, whatever that is, and are able to truly engage your consciousness in that activity while you are doing it—in other words, if you are passionate about your chosen activities, ice skating, roller blading, walking outside, gardening, whatever it is you love to do—that is enough for your soul. Treating the body well nourishes the soul, and a happy soul is essential to the experience of passion. Treating the body well affirms for your body that you respect it, that you honor it, and that's critical.

To be disconnected from feeling is to starve the soul and alienate the spirit, but it happens. We are, as people are so fond of saying, "only human." *Only human???* I don't know what's "only" about being an interdimensional creature with access to countless levels of consciousness, but I do know that someone's *mind* came up with that saying. It certainly did not originate with the body consciousness, which *has* no words, nor did the soul come up with it because the soul speaks through the heart, and it certainly did not come down from Spirit, which chose, out of every possibility in the universe, to embody in a human form. No, only a mind could come up with a demeaning phrase like "only human" because only the mind would be fool enough to belittle its own experience in the world.

If we are fortunate, we can use our minds in our own behalf or at least be smart enough to find someone to help us learn how to use our minds in our own behalf. If we are not so lucky, we will risk dragging around one very tired soul in this lifetime. We will also risk physical illness. And we will surely miss out on the experience of passion altogether.

Because of all this, loving what you do for a living is very important. Your work, whatever it is, affects your soul at a profound level. On a physical and an energetic level, your work affects your heart, both the organ that beats inside of you and the chakra that vivifies your life on earth. Because this area of the bagua, when seen as a life cycle, represents the cumulative wealth and wisdom of your life, it also, tangentially, affects your entire working life since it all leads inevitably to this point.

Linear time, as we know it, does not actually exist and, while it is a convenient device for ensuring that we all show up for the party at the same time, not ruining the surprise planned for a half an hour later, it does tend to skew what we think is reality. But what does that have to do with Relaxation and Rejuvenation?

Everything.

A few pages ago, I suggested that you regard this area of the bagua as "the future." I used the term "future" because it's very difficult for most people to wrap their heads around the idea that there isn't really any future ... no past either. Time is an aspect of something called the Time Space Continuum, of which you have no doubt heard or read. When ancient sages first posited the concept of living in the Now Moment, they may have known a whole lot more than we thought they knew, because the Now Moment is IT, the Now Moment is all there is, it's actually, really, all there is.

And we kind of know this. The "inner child" that psychologists have been going on about for decades is really there, except it's not so much "inner" as coexistent. The You that you see in the mirror every morning is just what your consciousness happens to be focusing on in the Now Moment. Also existing, also in Now Moments, is every other moment of your life ... and depending on how you view energy, all your lives. We are, after all, since energy can neither be created nor destroyed, multidimensional beings.

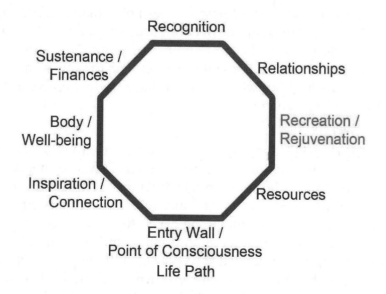

Recognition

Sustenance /
Finances

Relationships

Body /
Well-being

Recreation /
Rejuvenation

Inspiration /
Connection

Resources

Entry Wall /
Point of Consciousness
Life Path

Earlier I suggested that you might want to consider your future in terms of colors, and now I tell you that there is no future, that there's only Now, making your so-called future, Now as well so, really, you have more access to and influence on your so-called future than you might think. But try not to think too much; it's not really all that helpful when it comes to this stuff that used to be called "metaphysical" but which physicists are now "discovering" is pretty darn physical, after all. And most of the physicists can't wrap their heads around it either, so just let it go.

Your future, as it turns out, is your present ... and vice versa, making the previous suggestion even more critical because if your so-called future exists now then you have a very big hand in it (and, for that matter, your so-called future also has a hand in this Now Moment). You—and me, and everybody else—are a done deal ... but we're a constantly evolving done deal and you know who knows all about this and isn't the least bit confused by any of it and who will gladly walk you through it because that's its job? Your body. And you know why it can do all this? Because it doesn't think.

Because the language of the body is feelings (since the body doesn't think) what you can expect to experience and should pay attention to in dreams or when you awake on the morning after you do the assignment are feelings (as opposed to some kind of concrete information) and that's just fine because feelings are what really matter. Most of us are so led astray by being raised to "think" that we have come to rely almost totally on our minds—and the mind's constant sidekick, the Ego Process—for decision making, a real mistake because the job of the mind is, essentially, to make lists. The mind catalogues information. That's what it does, and it's good at it, but in the hierarchy of your being the mind is a functionary, nothing more.

What matters in life is how we feel, if we are content, or peaceful or happy. So if, after doing this assignment you awaken feeling elated, then you can feel justified—confident even—keepin' on keepin' on, just the way you are, no matter what that may look like to anyone else. If, on the other hand, you experience angst or sadness or fear, then pay attention because something is not right somewhere in your life. If you have suspicions about what might be amiss, make your own assignments up to get validation from your body, to make sure that you are on the right track. If you have absolutely no idea what could have caused the feelings, use an assignment to ask your body to please bring some useful hint or clue to the attention of your waking consciousness. (We'll explore creating your own assignments a bit later.)

Assignments for the Recreation and Rejuvenation Area of Your Life

Untapped Gifts and Potential

As I am reading this, I allow myself to feel gratitude to you, my wonderful body, for everything you do for me every day, breathing, circulating my blood and lymph, allowing the food I eat to nourish me, protecting me.

I notice how my body is feeling right now.

Now I picture myself asleep in bed tonight, knowing and understanding that you, my beloved body, will take over and put these words into action for me as I am sleeping, that I need to do nothing more than finish reading this.

I know that you know that we hold within us gifts that we have not yet realized. To the degree that it is comfortable for you and appropriate for us, I give you permission to release whatever may stand in the way of those gifts ripening, expanding, and becoming more useful to us.

In the morning I will take note of how I feel. Thank you for helping me to be all that I can be!

Here's an assignment that may help to put your mind in an open, imaginative, creative space:

As I am reading this, I allow myself to feel gratitude to you, my wonderful body, for everything you do for me every day, breathing, circulating my blood and lymph, allowing the food I eat to nourish me, protecting me.

I notice how my body is feeling right now.

Now I picture myself asleep in bed tonight, knowing and understanding that you, my beloved body, will take over and put these words into action for me as I am sleeping, that I need to do nothing more than finish reading this.

I know that you know that we hold within us gifts that we have not yet realized. To the degree that it is comfortable for you and appropriate for us, I give you permission to release whatever may stand in the way of those gifts ripening, expanding, and becoming more useful to us.

Thank you for helping me to be all that I can be!

Try this assignment on for size and feel what comes up for you on the following day:

Life Review

As I am reading this, I allow myself to feel gratitude (for something, anything).

I notice how my body is feeling.

Now I picture myself asleep in bed tonight, knowing and understanding that you, my beloved body, will take over and put these words into action for me as I am sleeping, that I need to do nothing more than finish reading this.

I know that you know what our whole life looks like at this moment. This is information that would be very useful to me—to us— in case my attention is needed to assist us in any way.

So to the degree that it is comfortable for you, I give you permission to release whatever might seem right and appropriate to let go of in order to allow me to have some waking conscious sense of the wholeness of our life.

You can fill any empty spaces that may be created by expanding the feeling I had when (you realized something important).

I honor you for helping me to help us be all that we can be.

Why I Am Here

As I am reading this, dear body, I allow myself to feel gratitude (for something, anything).

I notice how my body is feeling.

Now I picture myself asleep in bed tonight, knowing and understanding that you, my beloved body, will take over and put these words into action for me as I am sleeping, that I need to do nothing more than finish reading this.

111

I know that you know why we are here on Earth. I know that you know that I am unaware of this information. So I give you permission to release whatever you may need to release, to the degree that you are comfortable in doing so, in order to allow me to be more comfortable with trusting that your knowing is enough.

You can fill the empty space created by expanding the pleasure I feel when I am lost in a good story.

In the morning I will take note of how I feel. Thank you for helping me to be all that I can be!

Resources

Feng Shui

Well, we've made it just about full circle and are focused now on the eighth facet of the bagua which I call Resources. Resources and Connection have a lot in common in that they both relate to support. (If you think about it—something I don't often suggest, but, hey, it's fun sometimes—all four "corners" of the bagua octagon relate to support in some way. Connection offers the support of the invisible, Finances offers monetary support, Relationship offers people—probably the best support there is—and Resources offers book learning, among other things.

The Resources area, like Rejuvenation and Relaxation, has some built-in complexity, which is not surprising if you view the bagua in one of its many cyclic guises as following the flow of a lifetime. Conceived in the Life Path area, by the time you reach Resources, you have *become* a Resource, you are an elder. Your next step will be starting over again! So this area, while it refers to study of all sorts, to travel as a means to broadening your horizons and experiences of mankind, also refers to you as a resource for others. It refers to being mentored and to *being* a mentor. Resources is about gathering knowledge and experience so that you can be of use, so that you can give back.

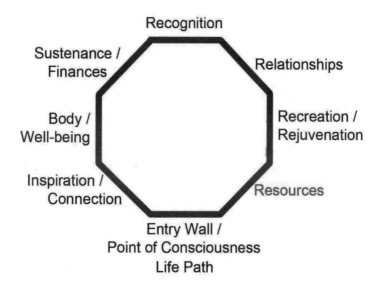

Because life is ever changing, learning is constant. We learn from our experiences, without a doubt, especially from new experiences, which is how this facet of the bagua came to be associated with travel, a hangover from the days when in order to learn something about another place or another culture you actually had to pick up and go there, a time when there were no photographs or films, when books were not as ubiquitous as they are today, and when illustrations had to be created by hand.

Then, as now, books are an invaluable resource. George Carlin once said, "If you go home with somebody and they don't have books, don't sleep with them." Well, OK, that's not quite what he said, but that's exactly what he meant. And what he was implying was that he, at least, didn't trust someone whose mind wasn't available and open to new information, and by new information I don't necessarily mean cutting-edge science, just things that you don't already know.

Inherent in this segment of the bagua is the proposition that if you don't take in information—about whatever interests you—then you have nothing to offer anyone else, which was essentially what George Carlin was saying.

Many people choose to place their books in this area of a room; the resonance is perfect. Certifications and diplomas and awards are well placed here. The elemental energy associated with Resources is Metal, so trophies or medals serve to activate the energy here too. And although all these things represent past achievements, just as in the R&R area, and for all reasons elaborated when I was mentioning the Space Time Continuum, they also promise your energy to a future where you share what you have learned.

If you actually like to read books, this facet of the bagua—energetically quiet as a rule because of its placement at the tail end of the energy flow—is a great place for a chaise or an armchair with some good lighting, creating a comfortable altar to reading where a bibliophile can settle in and read.

This area is also an appropriate place for hanging photographs of ancestors or teachers, icons, or people whose achievements you particularly admire. The Resources area reminds us of the best that humanity has to offer and, like the Connections area, wraps us back into a larger fold.

Sleep Magic

As mentioned previously, the energy of the Resources area is generally peaceful, meditative, even. In the cycle of the day, this area represents the first half of the night; in the cycle of the seasons, it is late fall/early winter; in the span of a human life, it is what some might refer to as the declining years. As a person who has assisted folks in crossing over for almost thirty years I can tell you that although the exterior of the body may seem to be declining, what is going on in the cellular intelligence of the body is just as active as ever, accounting for the thoughtful recognition among tribal cultures of what was called the elders.

Traditionally, elders are the wisdom keepers of a tribe because they've seen it all and lived through a lot of it. Their advice is usually offered, not dictated, because they know how advice is greeted, especially when it conflicts with a mind that has been made up.

The quiet space of the Resources area is reflective of your body's wisdom and intelligence and resonates powerfully with the work that is Sleep Magic in which you surrender the workings of your mind, with all its doubts and preconceptions, to the timeless knowledge of your body, allowing guidance to come from the profound connection that your body has with the Now Moment.

The mind—the Ego Process—is, as a rule, loathe to give up any of its power. That said, the mind is also easily duped and as trainable as it could be simply by using a "Look! Over there!" strategy that is commonly called mindfulness. Sleep Magic comes easy because you—and your very intelligent, overactive mind—are sound asleep, leaving the body to run its kingdom on its own. Extending the purview of your body's wisdom into your waking hours, however, takes a little work. It's not dreadfully hard work, though, I promise. All it requires is you paying attention; this is also known as mindfulness.

That's it, you paying attention to what you are doing.

It's a little more difficult than you might think because minds are usually way busier than we even notice because we're so used to the constant chatter. Yet, once the skill of mindfulness is acquired, it becomes second nature. That's because for your body, paying attention is its *first* nature. Paying attention is what bodies do.

When you are, say, driving, is all you are doing, driving? Is your mind totally engaged in scanning the road and what is up ahead of you, paying attention to what can be seen in your rearview mirrors, to the other cars in the nearby vicinity? "Oh, yes," you say, "it is!"

And is it doing anything else? Listening to the radio, maybe? Rehashing a conversation from the day before? Thinking about what's next on your schedule? It might be. In fact, it probably is. So you are not entirely paying attention to driving.

I'm not saying you *should* be, because that would be me telling you what to do (as well as the pot calling the kettle black), I'm just pointing out that paying attention to the one thing you are doing—in this case, driving—is not that simple because in this day and age what we do is not that simple, usually because we are doing many things at once.

But washing dishes is pretty simple, no?

Maybe not. Maybe you're looking out the window or having a conversation or listening to the radio or television or a conversation in the next room. My point is that if you at least try to focus on the one thing that you have set out to do you will begin to get your mind used to limiting itself to one topic at a time; you will, therefore, be improving its ability to focus. Multitasking does not bring the body peace and it hampers its ability to bring your mind peace, and when I say peace what I am talking about is a condition of significantly reduced stress.

Stress releases something called cortisol into the body. Cortisol breaks down the body. Cortisol ages the organs of the body. Anything you can do to simplify your life will reduce stress levels and since life comes with stressful challenges that you have no control over whatsoever, taking control where you can, helps. Give peace a chance. Try paying attention to exactly what you are doing. Live to be an elder.

Assignments for the Resources Area of Your Life

Here's a little assignment that will help you on your way to surrendering to your body's wisdom:

As I am reading this, I allow myself to feel gratitude (for something, anything).

I notice how my body is feeling.

Now I picture myself asleep in bed tonight, knowing and understanding that you, my beloved body, will take over and put these words into action for me as I am sleeping, that I need to do nothing more than finish reading this.

I know that you know why we are here on Earth. I know that you know that I don't know. So I give you permission to release whatever you may need to release, to the degree that you are comfortable in doing so, in order to allow me to be more comfortable with trusting that your knowing is enough.

You can fill the empty space created by expanding the pleasure I feel when I am lost in a good story.

In the morning I will take note of how I feel. Thank you for helping me to be all that I can be!

The following assignment is designed to prepare you to resonate with the highest vibrational version of yourself:

As I am reading this, I allow myself to feel gratitude to you, my body, for all that you have done for me throughout the course of this day.

I notice how you are feeling, and I give you permission to relax as we are reading this, allowing the words to sink deeply into the cellular consciousness of our body.

Now I picture myself asleep in bed tonight, knowing and understanding that you, my beloved body, will take over and put these

words into action for me as I am sleeping, that I need to do nothing more than finish reading this.

I know that we carry within our cells what might be called our future self. I am prepared to resonate more perfectly with that self and so, you have my permission tonight to let go—to the degree that you are comfortable—of any old programming that might stand in the way of that desire.

You can fill the empty space its leaving creates by expanding those aspects of us that are already heading in the direction of a higher, clearer vibration.

Thank you for helping me to become more truly all that I am.

Combined Baguas

When we first got acquainted with the bagua map, I mentioned that in many rooms you might well be placing the bagua in two different directions. Let's explore that today because those rooms where a double placement is most likely are some of the most used rooms in your house.

Just to refresh your memory, the first placement of the bagua will always be with the Life Path area lined up on the center of the Entry Wall to the room. The Life Path area will always be the center of that wall so the door to the room might fall in either the Resources or Connection areas as well. All three areas have a place on the Entry Wall.

The second bagua placement will be wherever someone—let's say it's you—is spending large blocks of time. For practice, let's imagine that it's your bedroom.

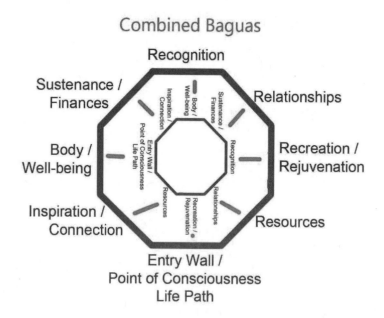

Combined Baguas

Recognition

Sustenance / Finances

Relationships

Body / Well-being

Recreation / Rejuvenation

Inspiration / Connection

Resources

Entry Wall / Point of Consciousness Life Path

The larger, outside bagua represents the layout of the room itself while the small, angled bagua within represents the placement of the bagua from the point of view of a person in the bed in the room. The room of course, is not octagonal, but rectangular.

The Point of Consciousness (aka Life Path)—the head of the bed—falls approximately in the middle of the left wall of the room giving the bed the double influence of Life Path and Health and Well-being, which feels like a good place for a bed to be since a good night's sleep is so much a part of good health. A beautiful, lush landscape would harmonize both with the Wood element of the Well-being area and with the Water element of the Life Path/Point of Consciousness area. Lush growth is always an apt metaphor for health and well-being.

The area just to the left of the Entry door to the space is a combination of the Resources area (from the bed) and the Inspiration/Connection area (from the Entry Wall). As mentioned before, both areas relate to support so the combination is natural and easy and a likely spot for pictures of the person or people who share the room, power animals, or possibly a mountain, which would resonate with the earth element of the Connection area as well as the metaphorical and geographical connection between mountains and wisdom (Resources).

Directly across from that, on the opposite side of the bed, the combined areas in that corner of the room are Inspiration/Connection (from the bed placement) and Finances (from the main placement of the bagua). Here, the combination of elemental energies are earth and wood which are not considered to be compatible; however, an image of a growing tree, preferably blossoming or fruiting, would show the potential for harmony between the elements while beautifully illustrating the concept of abundance.

Well-being and Recognition pair up in the center of the far wall. Because of the window—which also takes a bite out of the previously mentioned corner, this area is reduced in

121

size so whatever is hung on the wall here should be on the small side yet, ideally, very visible. My suggestion would be a really excellent photograph of the person or the couple sharing the room, perfectly reflecting the energy of the Recognition area and ideally showing the person or couple to be in superlative health.

As we continue moving clockwise around the room, we come to a dresser situated in an area that falls under the double purview of Relationships and Finance—a perfect combination if this is the room of a committed couple! Many phrases and metaphors likening a fulfilling relationship to a treasure come to mind, all of which could be brought to life in images or statuary. A lady's dresser in a Finance area is also a fabulous and fun place to have costume jewelry on display along with images (metaphorical or actual) of the couple or each other.

A single person, open to the idea of entertaining a relationship, needs to address in this area not the lack of said relationship, nor anything that would even remind one of a relationship, but rather that person's relationship with him or herself. Self-love—real appreciation for exactly what is—generates a beautiful and attractive vibration. You know who you are; celebrate that in the Relationship area, especially if that area is linked to the Finance area as it will activate that corner of the room bringing the opportunity to truly thrive.

Recognition (from the placement of the bed) and Recreation and Rejuvenation (from the basic placement of the bagua) mark the center of the wall just opposite the bed. Here, too, a picture of the room's occupant/s would be well placed as would any representations of peaceful togetherness with each other or with nature! Remember that the Recreation and Rejuvenation speaks to your future, so you can imagine too how you might like that to feel. Because this Recreation and Rejuvenation area is shared with Recognition, I'd avoid abstract art in this particular place. Recognition requires specifics, and the metaphoric aspects of abstract art are far too stimulating for a bedroom!

The next corner we come to, to the right of the entry door, brings together Resources and Relationships, another nice combination. In a couple's bedroom, this combination speaks of the potential for growing old together. There's a dresser top here too. On it, childhood pictures would appropriately speak to the wisdom of your years. You have been learning since before you were born ... and before you were four years old, you knew everything about what this life would bring you. Now you are here. Respect your journey and, if you are part of a couple, respect your journey together as well.

When we reach the middle of the Entry Wall, we've come full circle to the Life Path area, which is colored by the Recreation and Rejuvenation area from the standpoint of the bed. Doorways allow the interior energy of the house to flow into the space. In a bedroom, in a Life Path area, that is quite enough to be going on. Just ensure that the door works well and can be locked securely.

If your bedroom happens to be laid out just this way, lucky you! Your work's all done for you. If not, use a couple of transparent baguas and see what kinds of combinations you're working with, then go back and review each section on the bagua. Remember, this combining of bagua energies can happen in any room where you may be stationary for some time. (Remember too that even though there's been a lot of talk about wall-hanging art, things that sit on the floor fall into the areas too!)

Have fun!

Here's an assignment designed to assist you in your learning process:

As I am reading this, I allow myself to feel gratitude to you, my wonderful body, for everything you do for me every day, breathing, circulating my blood and lymph, allowing the food I eat to nourish me, protecting me.

I notice how my body is feeling right now.

Now I picture myself asleep in bed tonight, knowing and understanding that you, my beloved body, will take over and put these words into action for me as I am sleeping, that I need to do nothing more than finish reading this.

Dear body, I know that you know that we have taken in an awful lot of information in the past few weeks. This information matters to me and I would very much like to know it right down to my bones. So tonight I give you permission to release whatever seems right and appropriate to you to let go of that might be standing in the way of my really absorbing what I have learned.

Thank you, dear body. You are my absolute best friend.

Creating Your Own Sleep Magic Assignments

The following list of questions is taken from the work I do in my private practice. Most of our challenges in life have their roots in places that we have no conscious connection with, their tendrils reaching out and clasping onto places where old energy has coalesced in the subconscious and in the cellular structure of the physical body, forming small energetic blocks that may one day turn into disease, disability, money problems, relationship issues, or other life challenges.

Your answers to the following questions will give you a reliable and broad scan of your awareness of yourself. It will also alert your Ego Process to your intention to do some personal work. Because of that, it will be useful to you to take a moment, prior to answering the questions, to sit quietly, shut your eyes, and let your Ego Process know that it may feel a little uncomfortable with the Q&A but that you are doing it to increase your comfort for the rest of your life together. If you know that you tend to be defensive, in other words, if you know that your first answer to any question that might make you seem less than perfect is always going to be "No," then remind your Ego Process of that as well. It will at least allow you to catch yourself in the act!

I strongly recommend that you write your answers down on paper and that you leave a lot of room for afterthoughts to be added later.

Questionnaire

1. Are there situations that cause you to be afraid?
In some situations, of course, fear is a useful thing; it is a feeling, after all, that is designed to keep you from danger, designed to keep

you alive. Other times—like the fear of speaking in public, or fly-ing—the fear has been generated by some experience, even if the ex-perience was nothing more than hearing about something frighten-ing. In cases like those, where fear is actually holding you back from a full life, Sleep Magic can be used to address the issue as you give your body permission to release whatever is lying behind the fear.

2. Are there situations in which you feel insecure?

As with fear, most such situations have been generated by some-thing, and the underlying cause can be dismissed via Sleep Magic.

3. Do you sometimes lack concentration?

4. Are you easily distracted from your work?

5. Do you sometimes feel lonely?

6. In what situations can you be influenced/changed by others?

7. Do you worry more than is reasonable about the well-being of others?

8. Are you overly sensitive? If so, to what?

9. Do you tend to have a run-away mind?

   If so, is there a focus to your thoughts?

   If so, is there always one particular focus?

10. What makes you angry?

11. What is dissatisfying to you at the moment?

12. What makes you feel exhausted?

13. What keeps you from being completely happy?

14. Do you sometimes feel sad or blue?

15. Are you a perfectionist, or are you careless of de-tails?

16. Do you tend to have feelings of guilt?

17. Do you feel that you have been treated unfairly?

18. Is there something or someone that you cannot for-give?

19. Is there anything about which you are bitter?

20. Do you sometimes feel unclean?

21. How are you with decision making?

22. Are you more of an optimist or a pessimist?

23. How would you rate your self-esteem?

24. What do you do when other people have an opinion that is completely different from your own?

25. How would you react if you had to do something you resented with all your heart?

26. How do you react to unpleasant things?

27. Do you like to be comforted when you are sad?

28. What do you worry about?

29. Have you ever been without hope? Have you ever felt resigned to something? Did you ever in your life just give up?

30. Are there situations in which you react intolerantly?

31. What annoys you the most?

32. If you know any of the details surrounding your mother's pregnancy with you or your birth, please note them even if they seem silly or nonsensical.

33. Are there any outstanding instances of trauma (physical, psychological, or spiritual) that happened to you or to someone who played a significant role in your life that you still recall quite clearly?

34. What would you most like to change about yourself?

Once you finish answering these questions, you may have quite of lot of fodder for creating your very own assignments. Wherever your answers seem troublesome to you, that's a clue that your body may be holding onto something that it would like to let go of.

To create your assignments you can use the following #1, #2, and #3 segments from the *Creating Your Own Assignments* section just as they are … or you can make up wording that suits you better. As long as you get the points that are expressed in those sections across, the assignment will be perfectly set up.

The assignments are carefully worded to provide the best results, and by using the same format over and over again, you allow your body to grow ever more comfortable with the process. Once you've been doing assignments for a full month, your body will have begun to set a pattern in place because in that time the moon will have come full circle.

When it comes to the #4 segment, the actual request, if you are letting go of something quite specific—like a fear that you may have felt sometime—you can ask your body to release that fear specifically. If, however, you *don't* know what it is that you need to let go of, then you'll need to approach the wording of the assignment differently. For instance, let's say that you have a relative that annoys you and you'd really like not to be annoyed by that person. You may think that you know why that person annoys you (and you may be right) but you can't know for sure that that's all there is to it, so approaching your body by giving it permission to release whatever it is that you are holding onto that *causes* that annoyance would be a more effective way to proceed.

The same holds true if something unpleasant happened to you and you want things like that to never happen again. You'll need to give the body permission to let go of whatever it is inside you that *attracted* the unpleasant event. And you always want to give the body permission to let go of *only* what it is comfortable releasing. Your body had its reasons for holding onto whatever it is, and they may be very good reasons, so you want to be gentle and proceed slowly.

For #5, filling up the empty space created so the body doesn't feel empty, try to recall a time when you felt an opposite way to the feeling you want to let go of and allow your body to expand the good feeling. If you can't think of anything, then just give your body permission to expand whatever it feels is right and appropriate.

The last step, #6, is always gratitude. Say thank you with all your heart in whatever way seems good to you, and you can't go wrong.

Anatomy of a Sleep Magic Assignment

The following assignment is from a series of Life Before Life assignments in the book, *Sleep Magic: Surrender to Success*, available from Amazon or Barnes & Noble on line. Let's break the assignment down into its component parts.

1. *As I am reading this, I allow myself to feel gratitude to you, my wonderful body, for everything you do for me every day, breathing, circulating my blood and lymph, allowing the food I eat to nourish me, protecting me.*

Every assignment starts with thanking your body for the work it does for you. This can be simple or as thorough a thanking as you like. Sincerity is the most critical ingredient as you are consciously acknowledging and connecting with your body much as if it were another person with whom you wanted to be in a relationship. The goal of the gratitude that opens and closes every assignment is to lay down a foundation for mutual respect and trust.

2. *I notice how you are feeling and give you permission to relax as we read this, allowing these words to deeply penetrate your consciousness.*

This simply asserts that you are, right now, at this moment, paying attention to your body as you take the next step forward in your relationship, expressing your desire that your body be comfortable because you care about this relationship. The more relaxed your physical body is, the more "attention" it pays to words.

Essentially, it's enough to simply notice the tension or relaxation in your body and expand the feeling of relaxation.

> 3. *Now I picture myself asleep in bed tonight, knowing and understanding that you, my beloved body, will take over and put these words into action for me as I am sleeping, that I need to do nothing more than finish reading this.*

I refer to this as "the snapshot." It allows your body to have a visual image, strengthening the timing of your request. Even if you are not a visual person, even if you do not "see" things in your mind's eye, the body knows what to do with this information which is as much about *feeling* as it is about a visual image ... and, in fact, feeling is enough. I supply the words for those who have difficulty connecting with their bodies.

> 4. *I know that there is some chance that our mother's endometrium may have rejected us at first. Even now, rejection doesn't feel so good. If this happened, I give you permission, to the degree that you are comfortable in so doing, to release any feelings of fear or desperation that may have accompanied that period in our life.*

The first three parts of the assignment can be the same every time you do the work but at #4 everything gets far more specific and individualized. This particular assignment deals with an issue (the fact that the embryo may not have attached securely right away) that may or may not have occurred. If it did not, the body will simply pass the assignment by.

At #4 you are presenting the body with your request, be that for a release, an expansion or simply to have something brought to your conscious attention. Here, the words are absolutely necessary and should be carefully chosen, avoiding words like "not" and "no," which mean nothing to the body.

5. *You can fill the empty space their leaving (the old energies, that is) may create by expanding the way I feel when I have felt welcomed _____. (Here, you would fill in the blank with something specific that you had, at one time, experienced.)*

To do nothing but release, release, release, night after night, would leave your body energetically depleted. Ideally, when you give the body permission to expand something after a release you draw upon your own past history for a feeling that feels opposite to that which you are asking to release. Tying the energy—the feeling you are asking the body to expand—to a specific event from your own life makes for a more potent energy even if the event was a small one. If you have nothing to suggest, then simply give your body permission to expand whatever it feels would be right and appropriate to fill the empty space.

6. *I honor you for helping me to feel safe and comfortable in the world.*

We open with gratitude and we close with it. You can be as flowery as you like, as I often am, or you can just issue a heartfelt thank-you. Your body, which most likely hasn't heard enough good about itself in its lifetime, will be most appreciative and grow ever more willing to help you because you are helping your body, with every step, to have a more comfortable life as well.

Sweet sleep!

13
Detailing

Life is filled with distractions and just as those distractions can interfere with the efficient functioning of your mind, adding stress to your life, so too can they interfere with the Feng Shui of your space. There are distractions creating compromised Feng Shui lurking in the living and working spaces of most people. They are the "little things" that need fixing or adjusting or tossing that don't get fixed or adjusted or tossed. The reason that they bother the Feng Shui of a space is threefold: (1) good Feng Shui requires that things be clean (no old energy building up), (2) in good repair (what is supposed to work, should work, out-of-order appliances carry the energy of things not working in your life), and (3) pleasing to behold (unattractive things tell you that your life is ugly).

When things are dirty, they become energetically heavier. Feeling the greasy build-up of anything in a kitchen that hasn't been cleaned recently actually causes the body to recoil slightly because "dirt" anywhere near food is not usually conducive to the well-being of the body. That small response causes an energetic insult to the body, and the Ego Process sometimes responds by judging you for bad housekeeping. None of this helps your inner Feng Shui, which of course rebounds right into the Feng Shui of your space.

Dust on surfaces and the particulate that falls out of the air in or near big cities gets a similar response from the body, particularly the lungs. Dust doesn't look good either, dulling the natural shine of curtains and furniture, all the while quietly pointing out to your body that all that stuff is going into your lungs—which it is, and well before it lands on your furnishings. Your lungs, if they are healthy, are designed to deal with normal amounts of airborne particles, no problem, but the constant reminder of thin layers of dust plays heavily on the mind, which excels at making mountains out of mole-hills, again disturbing your internal Feng Shui and potentially weakening your resistance because your mind has quite a bit to do with your physical well-being.

Spots on carpets, mold on tiles, threads hanging from bedspreads or curtains, broken blinds, torn screens, chipped furniture ... the list goes on and on and all of it creates a mild level of annoyance that is energetically disturbing, albeit at a very low level ... but things add up and that's the real problem. Your living space—your nest—is supposed to be the place you can look to for soothing at the end of the day, for inspiration at the beginning of the day. It's supposed to provide you with the comfort you crave. That's what good Feng Shui does. Anything that detracts from that state of mind is a detriment to the aura of well-being that is the goal of Feng Shui. Couched in comfort you can greet what life brings you with equanimity; annoyed by loose ends, there's a low-level vibration of frazzle that can interfere with your composure.

Now perhaps you are a person who isn't bothered by such picayune things as greasy teapots or moldy showers; the thing is, your body is bothered. Our bodies are orderly and they run on schedules; they love routine and a healthful diet. You may think that you can slip a lot past them when you are young but it all adds up, relentlessly compromising the good work the body does for you until you become all too aware that your body just isn't working as it used to. Your body likes and responds well to order because *it* is orderly in its habits and in its functions; it responds well to cleanliness because it requires that to stay healthy. "You" may not care that there's a red wine stain peeking out from under an arm-chair, but your body does. And even though its subtle responses may go unnoticed by you, since "you" live inside that body just as much as you live inside your space, your personal Feng Shui is compromised by the compromised Feng Shui of your home.

Think about walking through your space and making a list of the things that need to be done. Then get out a calendar and schedule them. There's no rush, just knowing that you've made the commitment—as long as you actually follow through!—will make a difference to your state of being and to your state of mind.

Collecting/Clutter

How much is too much?

When does collecting become cluttering?

When does clutter become hoarding, and what's going on there anyway?

We love our stuff. Most of us do, anyway. And if I had to pick between erring on the side of too much stuff or too little, I'd go with too much, for sure. But that's me ... and it's me with a lot of space. Me in a small space prefers the space. People have different tastes in everything including how they feel about and react to non-necessities in the home. Then there's the fact that one person's non-necessities are another's necessities. Again, it's a very individual matter.

But stuff can reach a tipping point and then it's called clutter. When there are too many things in a space to be able to see and appreciate the individual things, when you have to move things out of the way to see something else, or to put something else—like a cup or a glass that you are using—down, then you've hit that tipping point. When there's no open space on a side table, you don't need a table, you need a display case. When tchotchkes have rendered the flat surfaces of your home un-usable for anything else except their own display, something has to change because the energetic effectiveness of your space is being seriously compromised. You're being compromised in your own space! That should be a clue.

There are two ways you can go to get out of this energetic dilemma, and they both relate to the energy around the items in question. If you love them, really love them, if they mean something to you, find them a home of their own in a showcase or vitrine. Corralling numbers of items in one space makes them a collection and that can actually amplify the good energy in your space. Placed in the Finance area of a room it speaks directly to an abundance that matters to you. Placed in the Resources area, it identifies a passion of yours, something you know about, something people can know about you.

You can also perform triage on the items. This is useful when you actually do collect something—like elephant carvings or turtles or Hummel figurines—and over the years people who know you, and may have been stuck for a gift on a special occasion, have given you one of these items and you don't particularly like it. Holding onto things you have no attachment to, especially if you actively don't like them, is especially bad Feng Shui for both you and your space, reminding you every time you see the thing that you are doing something you don't want to do; that generates more of that feeling energy for you. The next time someone admires the thing, give it to them. Or ship it off to a nonprofit secondhand shop. In keeping with the item having been a gift, do not sell it, give it away.

"But what will I tell the person who gave it to me?" Tell them the truth, carefully phrased. Tell them that a dear friend fell in love with it and that you gave it to them. Or tell them that you had to scale down and let go of a number of things, that you were sad about that (sad that you had to scale down) but it had to be done.

Collections, even when corralled, can unbalance Feng Shui, particularly if the collection is of an animal of some sort. Birds and fish and animals carry a lot of symbolic energy on their own; it's why we're attracted to them. In many ethnic traditions, it is thought that each of us has our own power animal and that if we lose touch with that we become ill. It is wiser, from a Feng Shui standpoint, to have only one representation—or a few, at most—of any animal in your home,

135

lest its primary characteristics be amplified out of proportion. (Of course, if you should happen to actually have a representation of your power animal, that is best kept in your bedroom, and not open to public display.)

The extreme condition of clutter, hoarding, in severe cases, often doesn't appear to be as cluttered as plain old clutter does because very frequently people who hoard are quite orderly about their stash. Behind hoarding lies a deep-seated fear about not having enough; a sense of not having control over the vagaries of life leads to the need to control whatever can be controlled so, as a rule, although the person has way more of whatever it is that they've focused on—and sometimes there's no focus at all—they keep it arranged in such a way so as to make it easily accessible because they might need it. It's important to know what you've got if you are constantly concerned that you might not have enough.

Hoarding is a symptom of a psychological issue and needs to be addressed tactfully and, ideally, with professional help. Sleep Magic too can be of assistance. It is, of course, the person who needs the help first, before the space does, as you cannot deprive someone who feels that they need a lifeline of that lifeline without possibly causing serious emotional damage.

Just to help clear out your internal clutter, let's have another pre-birth assignment:

As I am reading this, I allow myself to feel gratitude for all the many ways you, my dear body, help to keep us comfortable and functional.

I notice how you are feeling, and I give you permission to relax as we are reading this, allowing the words to sink deeply into the cellular consciousness of our body.

Now I picture myself asleep in bed tonight.

I know that you remember the moments after our birth. If during that time our mother may have felt in any way unclean or dirty and passed that sense on to us, to the degree that it is comfortable for you, I give you permission to let it go.

You can fill the empty space its leaving may create by expanding the way I feel just after a bath or shower.

Thank you for helping me to feel the light that I know I carry.

The Ego Process and the External Observer

The Ego Process

There's no way around it: we all have egos. I usually refer to the ego as the Ego Process, that way it's more identifiable as what it really is, a function of the mind as it tries to make its way in the world. The Ego Process starts early, probably as soon as we begin to recognize that we have a separate identity, and it continues developing—and changing—throughout life.

It is the recognition of our separateness that requires us to develop an ego because as a child we need to know who—and how—to be with whom, in order to get what we want/need. This is a critical skill for any child. As children our lives are dependent upon our caretakers, and we must learn early how to manipulate our behavior to please these large people who seem to be in charge of our lives.

Those who master the art usually grow up to have a dependable, strong Ego Process, one that works well for them in that it helps them to get where they want to go while at the same time not offending—and possibly even assisting—those around them. Those who do not master the skill or who were repeatedly denied or shut down as children tend to fall at the ends of the Ego Process spectrum and become either overbearing or underwhelming. (Something, by the way, that can be neatly handled with Sleep Magic assignments targeted on letting go of whatever led to the current condition.)

In childhood, the Ego Process is necessary for survival because it is focused on the needs of the individual. Because most neural connections are firmly established before the age of seven, so too is the nature of the Ego Process. Lacking any kind of self-consciousness or self-awareness, the nature of the

Ego Process will remain the same well into adulthood despite the fact that for most of us, by adulthood our relationship to survival has dramatically changed because as mature individuals, we are in charge of our lives (to the degree that anyone can be in charge of anything).

The result of this continuity is that a good many supposedly "grown-up" people are walking around on the earth with an Ego Process that is still firmly anchored in its childhood world, still bowing to whatever constraints were in place then, still reveling in the occasional pat on the head from an authority figure, still gloating over getting picked first or lamenting over getting picked last, unable to maintain a neutral stance and embrace the knowledge that everything is—always—exactly as it should be.

It's essential to know where you stand with your Ego Process. There's a bumper sticker I've seen that says "Question authority"; well, the Ego Process thinks that it is your inner authority so ideally you'll take a moment to question yourself even about what may seem on the face of it to be "good" decisions. "Where did this come from? Is this the grown-up, adult me making this choice, or is it some other aspect of me?"

It's helpful to know why you act as you do because knowing what lies behind your actions will open you up to the kind of self-awareness that is invaluable for real clarity. This is precisely the sort of thing that Sleep Magic assignments can help you sort out because your body does not fall under the sway of your mind or your Ego Process while you are sleeping; your body has an authority—and a language—all its own. The authority of the body is what you might call Spirit—whatever ineffable force vivifies the animal body you inhabit—and the body's language is feelings. While you can always question what you think, what you feel is not usually questionable; the body, unlike the mind, does not doubt or second guess itself.

Animals are pure beings, unsullied by the machinations of a mind, and your body *is* an animal. Its very purity allows

139

it the kind of connection to Spirit that we thinking beings have to strive to attain through such practices as meditation or yoga. And just as Spirit "picks" our parents, it picks the body we inhabit as well; the connection between Spirit and body is intimate and if we desire to live a life guided by Spirit, it is in our best interest to surrender the processes of the ego to scrutinization by the body. Sleep Magic is a way to do that.

The External Observer

In the quest for self-improvement, nothing is more useful than self-awareness.

The Ego Process influences every aspect of your waking conscious mind; it cannot be otherwise. And the Ego Process, as we've seen, is not all troublesome. Some aspects of it can be quite helpful and even mature. The brain, once thought to be almost locked into its way of functioning after adolescence, is now known to have great plasticity as we age. So in addition to the large bulk of programmed information from childhood we also have a great deal of very helpful, very sensible information gleaned from our adult experiences and reinforced by years of repetition. It is this information that can be relied on to help us become everything we are.

The Ego Process is not by nature self-aware; it is, rather, a spontaneous and immediate function that springs into action triggered by the emotional tone of whatever events are going on. But, much like a very large puppy dog, it is trainable, and requiring it to develop what I call an External Observer will prove to be one of the most useful tools you have in your transformation toolbox. An External Observer can be useful in assessing in a very nonjudgmental way both your behavior and the spaces in which you live and work, allowing you to make subtle changes that can yield obvious results.

When you are training a puppy, consistency is essential, so when you say, "Sit," and the puppy doesn't, you gently push its hindquarters toward the floor as you repeat the command. You do that as often as is necessary for the small beast to catch on. If the small beast is going to grow up to be a very big beast—like your Ego Process!—then you simply cannot give up the training or it, not you, will be running the show.

To train your Ego Process to develop an External Observer you will need to be similarly consistent and equally *in*sistent. You will need to teach yourself to take a moment every now and then to mentally step back, gather as much objectivity as possible, and assess what has just happened. Pure objectivity is, of course, impossible, but since most of us have been raised to be aware of other people's needs (sometimes too much so!), you can turn that skill on yourself, imagining that you are someone else or, conversely, that your External Observer is someone else that just happens to be living in your brain, a someone else who is totally without judgment and sees clearly what has gone on.

Some people like to personalize their External Observers by imagining them as characters or creatures of some sort. One of my clients even went so far as to get his External Observer—a muppet-like creature as he described it to me—a girlfriend. Whatever it takes!

In the beginning, it may seem quite artificial, but just as the puppy incorporates its training, your External Observer will eventually become second nature. After seven years, when all of the existing cells in your body have caught on, the installation of your External Observer will be quite complete and very much a part of you.

I can just hear you now ... "Seven years! Seven years! What is she talking about, seven years? I thought this was all gonna be wrapped up tight a lot faster than that." Well, what's done in a day will be done in a day and what's done in a month will be done in a month, but the tools I am giving you are tools that can be used for the rest of your life and that will continue to serve you well because there is always better to get! If you are not improving yourself, you are going backward. Feng Shui, remember, is about the flow in life and it is

141

always changing, as are you. The bagua will serve you well as you shift and change the spaces around you to better support an ever-evolving you. Sleep Magic, allowing you, as it does, to continually refine yourself at deeper and deeper levels with little effort on your part, will also serve you well, and the more you use it, the more your life becomes a veritable treasure.

Change will begin right away; you'll feel it. But really profound changes will begin to occur, seemingly on their own, once your body has truly incorporated the nightly changes you are requesting and that take seven years just because it does. Despite all the advertisements of healing techniques promising you that you can change your life in thirty days or sometimes even thirty minutes, your body, your very physical, governed-by-the-laws-of-nature body, requires seven years to allow new information to penetrate every cell and only when change becomes that physical can it really be considered to be integral to your being. The "feeling" of change is nice but it is a feeling; actual change may not feel like any one thing in particular but it will be undeniably reflected in every aspect of your life and it's worth every moment that it takes to get to that place, the place where your embodied Spirit can really call home.

The following assignment is designed to assist you in laying a foundation for your own External Observer:

As I am reading this, dear body, I allow myself to feel gratitude for all the many ways you help to keep us comfortable and functional.

I notice how you are feeling and give you permission to relax as we read this, allowing these words to deeply penetrate your consciousness.

Now I picture myself asleep in bed tonight, knowing and understanding that you, my beloved body, will take over and put these words into action for me as I am sleeping, that I need to do nothing more than finish reading this.

I know that you know that I am working closely with you to raise our vibrational level, and I know you know that being able to be more self-aware will greatly assist in this.

So I give you permission now to release whatever seems right and appropriate to you to let go of so that we may easily develop our own External Observer, expanding the self-awareness we already have.

I honor you for helping me to be the best me I can be.

The Two Most Critical Rooms in Your House

The Kitchen

The kitchen is a place of nourishment and the perfect place to illustrate co-creation, to show that not only does your space affect you but that *you* affect it as well.

When we prepare food, even if that preparation is no more than lifting the lid from a microwaveable container (though I really hope not!), our energy goes into the food. In other words, we feed ourselves—and anyone else who may be sharing that food—our mood. Food prepared in a poorly lit space with countertops that beg for a cleaning is food that becomes tinged with the low level of dissatisfaction that is generated by working in such conditions. Likewise, food prepared with love tastes better than food prepared begrudgingly. Food consumed around contented, happy people is digested more easily than food consumed in an atmosphere of tension. All of this has been known since time immemorial.

The kitchen in any home is reflective of the health of the people who live there while in turn it affects that health and well-being in its innate efficiency, effectiveness, comfort level, and cleanliness. Is your kitchen clean? Is it organized efficiently? The body loves organization; it responds to order as a reflection of its own internal order. Is it easy to work in your kitchen? Struggling to find a good spot to work generates a low level of agitation that creates a mild energetic field of discomfort, which your body and the bodies of anyone else in that kitchen will register at an unconscious level, an energetic filed that will permeate every porous surface in that space from ceiling to floor and grow more dense with each passing day.

One of the easiest adjustments to make in a kitchen to make it a more Feng Shui compliant is to make sure that nothing sharp or pointy is on display. The appearance of knives and scissors triggers primal places in the brain that deal with self-defense. Remember, we are, first and foremost, animal creatures and as such, our most fundamental drive is survival and for millions of years our ancestors used pointy objects both to derive nutrition from the local fauna and to defend themselves from other humans encroaching on their territory. This primitive-sounding behavior has a lot more tenure in our DNA than does what we like to call *civilization*.

It is said that the prominent placement of visible knife blades in a kitchen leads to arguments, and I have received quite a lot of testimony to support that in my years of consultations. Those wooden blocks into which knives can be slid, blades out of sight, are a definite improvement, more so if discretely placed or slightly hidden.

Open trash cans are another source of downgraded energy and, thankfully, one sees fewer and fewer of those as Feng Shui gently begins to color mainstream thought. Good Feng Shui is all about creating balance and peace in a home, about creating a nest wherein one can weather the storms of life. An orderly, clean kitchen where all the appliances are working as they should, creates a strong center for that nest.

Critique your kitchen from the top down, inside and outside the cabinets, the appliances, under things, on top of things, and places you normally might not ordinarily see (like the top of the refrigerator). Make a list for yourself of what needs improvement. Walk that list over to your calendar and schedule the work that needs to be done according to the way that will actually work for you. If you are the type of person who dives into things, surfacing for air only when the job is complete, then set aside a day or a weekend for the work. If you are, rather, a person who can only take just so much cleaning, then schedule a task to do on each day that you have extra time available. Yes, it will take longer that way, but your mood matters! Know who you are and how you work best and schedule yourself accordingly and without judgment.

The Bedroom

Sleep Magic happens while you sleep, it happens inside the cellular consciousness of your body. Your body, of course, is inside something as well, presumably a living space of some sort. Because this place where you are sleeping is—especially now that you are (ideally) doing Sleep Magic every night—very important to your physical well-being, it's a good idea to take a critical look at that space.

The organs of the body replenish themselves as you sleep; all your cells do. Sleep—like food—is something that we need to get enough of in order to function properly. A person who sleeps poorly has a lower level of mental acuity than does a well-rested person, and a person who does not get as much sleep as he or she requires simply doesn't have the energy to exercise their body as it should be exercised to keep it in good working order.

One of the least followed tenets of excellent Feng Shui is a mirror-free bedroom. A bedroom should be mirror-free for a very good reason: bedrooms are supposed to be places of peace and stillness; mirrors bring a vibration very much the opposite of that, amplifying light energy in the space throughout the day and turning the bedroom into a kind of battery, buzzing with vibration when it should be a place of calm. Even a bedroom with a primarily northern exposure (and therefore less exposure to direct sunlight) loses some of its advantage when mirrors are present.

Direct exposure to a mirror while sleeping has been known to amplify disease processes in the body and in my own practice, in every case where I was called in because of terminal illness, the afflicted person had been sleeping directly across from a very large mirror, one that reflected the whole body. In retrospect, this had even been true in my own case in my pre-awareness-of-Feng-Shui days. It is most likely that in instances such as these the people in question were already seriously challenged in some way, but mirrors amplify energy, that's what they do, and if the energy is not good, then not-good energy is what gets amplified.

Most of us have grown up with a mirror in the bedroom and many people feel inconvenienced by not having one there, but there are ways around the ordinance. The easiest way is to have the mirror on the inside of a closet door but curtaining the mirror will work just as well. As long as the mirror is only exposed while it is being used and is denied the possibility of reflecting and amplifying light energy throughout the day, it will not prove troublesome.

Electrical energy is another known detriment to physical well-being as even the lowest wattage light gives off an electromagnetic field that can bother a vulnerable sleeping body at least a little. We are all more vulnerable when we sleep, to everything including toxins. Growing children and those compromised by any sort of organic physical challenge are even more vulnerable. I recommend, if you are interested in having a bedroom that supports health, obtaining a tri-field meter and learning how to use it. A tri-field meter will allow you to measure electromagnetic fields, seeing where they drop off, so that you can ensure that your bed is placed well away from potentially hazardous energy. (When using a tri-field meter, bear in mind that underground water can also create electromagnetic fields.)

The placement of your bedroom with regard to the direction of the light energy that affects it is also something to be aware of. If the windows in the room are facing south, they will be taking in light energy throughout the day. If you have difficulty sleeping or consistent health problems and a bedroom window that faces the south, you may want to consider keeping curtains or shades pulled throughout the day to limit that incoming energy.

A north-facing bedroom brings the opposite problem to those susceptible to oversleeping or sluggishness and is somewhat more difficult to address if no other bedroom is available. Such a conundrum may require an in-person consultation to see what natural resources may be on hand that can be worked with. One thing that may be useful is the use of a timed "dawn" clock, a light that comes on at very low wattage and grows brighter and brighter, usually over a period of about a half an hour. Placed in such a position that the light can shine on the eyelids of the sleeping person, this imitation of nature can sometimes train the body to follow nature's light cycles.

Bedrooms with east-facing windows are excellent for those who need help getting up in the morning. The energy of the east is a rising energy and lends a kick-start to the day. Those with a night job would do well to avoid a bedroom with east-facing widows! The west offers declining energy, usually resonant with very good rest, and it makes a great spot for most children's rooms, bringing their energy down a little. A bedroom with western light may be challenging for the elderly or ill, though, as it is not considered to be as "nourishing" as the rising energy of the east, but for the dying, it is just lovely.

Images in the bedroom should tend toward the peaceful and not toward the inspirational! Inspiration is a very active and energetic condition. Slogans and sayings that are meant to feed your mind have no place in a room where the mind is supposed to be still. If you want to send yourself messages on how to be in the world, send them in other rooms of the house. One very wise mother I encountered had her children create inspirational messages for themselves, which she then attached—at child-height eye level—to the doors in the house.

Photographs in the bedrooms of adults need to be only of those adults. The bedroom is a private space and for couples, it is a private and *intimate* space. Having photographs of other people in a bedroom with you is tantamount to having those people in bed with you … it's the eyes. The eyes really are the windows to the soul and subtle yet powerful connections are made through perfectly ordinary photographs.

Ideally, as mentioned in the Relationship chapter, in a couple's bedroom there will be at least one photograph or portrait of the couple together. Spring and summer landscapes are always appropriate. A picture of the place where the couple exchanged vows would be a deeply meaningful piece for the bedroom. Still-life paintings are better displayed in other rooms of the house as the goal of the bedroom is enhancing life itself and the vibrant physicality of the body. The same goes for abstracts of a more angular nature, though abstracts utilizing soft colors and shapes that seem to speak of a dream-like state or relaxation can work very well.

In the rooms of young children, pictures of the parents are desirable, reminding the child that his or her parents are there to support them. This is so right up to the point when the child wishes to not have that particular reminder, a sign that appropriate maturing is taking place.

The images in children's bedrooms need not be as peace-inducing as those in the rooms of adults, however, images that are too action oriented or that are scary in any way are best relegated to a playroom or den. Ideally, frightening images have no place in a home but children—especially adolescents—go through phases where they are processing life in very deep ways and to deny them that in their own home— the only place they have to truly feel safe and secure—is to risk leaving them with loose ends that may not be able to be secured at a later time.

Be as generous as you feel you can be with the strange needs of growing children while still attempting to keep their bedrooms as "sacred" places for their little bodies to thrive and grow.

A Word about Bathrooms

Bathrooms are where energy goes away. That's good. There are energies that need to go away. Don't concern yourself, though, that having a bathroom in any particular area of the bagua is taking energy away from that part of your life. If the bathroom is clean, efficient, and functioning well then it is doing exactly what it is supposed to be doing, and that is good Feng Shui.

The presence of a bathroom may signify that there is somewhat more activity than you might care for in that arena of your life, but it's a very rare thing when a bathroom is so large that it takes up entirely one whole segment of the bagua. But even if it does, a properly functioning, clean bathroom is a good and a wonderful thing. Make it look beautiful in whatever way suits your taste so that while you are in the room, you are glad to be there. Remember, your energy feeds the space every bit as much as it feeds you.

Do pay attention to the ventilation. If there is a window, have it open at least a little when the weather makes that a possibility; if there is a ventilation fan, use it when necessary, especially after baths or showers. A liquid paraffin candle in an attractive holder is an ideal accessory for every bathroom as the flame burns off untoward odors and energies. Liquid paraffin has the added benefit of not "painting" the walls with a light layer of soot which regular candles always do. (In fact, if you burn candles for hours in any room of the house, you would be wise to wash the walls at least once a year as that soot binds old energies to the walls.)

Treat the bathroom as a world unto itself if it troubles you, and keep the door to it closed. If possible, find something beautiful to hang on the outside of the door, facing your main living space. If your bathroom is a wonderland then, by all means, leave the door open a bit—preferably not enough to show off the toilet or bidet—and let it seem like a door to a delightful spa.

This assignment takes you back to your first bedroom:

As I am reading this, I allow myself to feel gratitude to you, my wonderful body, for everything you do for me every day, breathing, circulating my blood and lymph, allowing the food I eat to nourish me, protecting me.

I notice how you are feeling and give you permission to relax as we read this, allowing these words to deeply penetrate your consciousness.

Now I picture myself asleep in bed tonight, knowing and understanding that you, my beloved body, will take over and put these words into action for me as I am sleeping, that I need to do nothing more than finish reading this.

I know you recall how it felt becoming free of the zona pellucida after we made it into our mother's uterus and how we floated about for a while, looking for a place to settle. I cannot imagine how that must have felt to you but if it was in any way disturbing, you have my permission, to the degree that you are comfortable in so doing, to release the feelings now as we have no need to carry them around.

You can fill the empty space their leaving may create by expanding the way I feel when I get all cozy _____.

I honor you for helping me to feel safe and comfortable in the world.

Sleep Magic for the Advancing Soul

Compassion

There's always better to get ... and none of us will ever
be perfect ... except that we are always exactly perfect just as
we are at any given moment. Sometimes a person, meaning
to be of assistance, will ask you if what you are doing is really
on your path or he or she might congratulate you for being
on your path but the fact is that we are all, always, on path,
right where we need to be doing just what we need to be doing. It could not be otherwise, so the term, "the Advanced
Soul," is really a kind of a joke because a soul is a soul is a
soul, each of us remarkably individual, each with our own
interdimensional histories, each perfect. Each one of us a
mere speck on a planet that is a mere speck in a universe that
is a mere speck in a cosmos that ... well, you get the idea.

Every one of us is a cosmos unto ourselves. Your body
is the universe for all the infinitesimally small components of
the cells that make up your body, components that may have
as much submicroscopic life on their surfaces and inside
them as the earth has visible life on and inside its surface. The
best we can do for ourselves and for the immense life form of
which we are a part is to be the best that we can be, to be in
our integrity.

That means that "perfect" is a changeable designation
because we are constantly in the process of becoming and
there is always more perfect to get. Sleep Magic is a flawless
instrument for the never-ending, always-ascending journey
that is life. You will find as your experience of life becomes
more and more comfortable, that your heart will almost au-
tomatically expand its embrace, that the compassion you

hold in your heart will desire to expand. This happens because the more you grow to embrace yourself just as you are and the more you truly love yourself without any judgment, the more you can feel, at a cellular level, that everyone deserves to feel as good as you do and you will wish that for them, all the while knowing that they may not be ready for such a thing and that all you can do is to love them, just as they are.

Once upon a time, in a transmission from my father after his death, I received some of the most valuable information I have ever heard: *the people who love you the most in Spirit are the people who will hurt you the most in your life on earth, risking your hatred in a physical existence where love matters so much in order to provide you with what you need to become the person you have come to earth to be.*

People who hurt other people, who hurt children, have been hurt themselves. They deserve our compassion, not our resentment. They need not be a part of your life, for that may not even be wise, but they do merit agape.

As you become more compassionate you will desire to lose the automatic judging of others that springs so easily from the machinations of an overactive Ego Process that is always seeking to pat itself on the head, always looking to be better than others so that it can please its long gone mommy or daddy, always noticing when someone else is behaving badly or dressed poorly, too fat or too skinny or too perfect.

You might want to make use of the following assignment on a monthly basis so that you can become even more the self that you came here to be:

As I am reading this, I feel gratitude to you, dear body, for all the many ways you help to keep us comfortable and functional.

I notice how you are feeling right now, and I give you permission to relax as we read this, allowing these words to deeply penetrate our cellular consciousness.

Now I picture us asleep in bed tonight, knowing and understanding that you, my beloved body, will take over and put these words into action for me as I am sleeping, that I need to do nothing more than finish reading this.

I know that you know that I am sometimes judgmental of others, and that that trait is useless to me. I would rather be filled with a love for myself that is so much a part of me that what I always project onto others will be love.

To that end, I give you permission now to release whatever seems right and appropriate to you to let go of so that we may become a truly compassionate being.

I honor you for helping me to be the best me I can be.

Contentment

Most of us have been raised with the concept that "more" and "bigger" are better. As a look around any large gathering of people at a mall or large department store will easily illustrate, "more" and "bigger" have taken us to a place that isn't as good as it might be. The stores are filled—overfilled—with items that are simply unnecessary, trivial things whose creation uses up critical natural resources, and many of the people in the stores, there to purchase these superfluous items, have overindulged themselves nutritionally as well. The United States in particular is an overweight nation, fed on food products that have been designed to do little more than taste good.

Something is missing in the life of a person who always wants "more" and that something is contentment. But in a land where the chief goal of even many new-age and purportedly spiritually oriented educational materials is how to get what you want, what else might we expect? Always wanting what we do not have, always striving to reach goals that involve things outside of ourselves, all the while not paying attention to or reveling in what we actually *do* have is bound to create a void but that void can never be filled by anything that is outside of the self.

I trust that you noticed my use of the phrase "reveling in"; I chose that phrase for a very specific reason, and it's because gratitude, while it is essential to the balance of life, does not necessarily carry joy with it and it does not have to carry contentment. It is quite possible to be almost clinically grateful, grateful that we have what we have but, oh, all the things we don't have, all the things we want … and it is wanting that creates the void.

Sometimes, too, we have things—situations, usually— that we don't want, diseases or problematic relationships or parts of a job that we don't like, and we are rarely grateful for those things even though we often discover, in retrospect, that they may have changed us for the good in some way or opened our minds. Not wanting things that you do have does not create a void, but it does put the energy of the body at risk and stresses an immune system that can do nothing for you because these unwanted situations are the work of Spirit. They are your personal challenges to be dealt with.

Consider, if you have such an aspect to your life, using a Sleep Magic assignment to assist you in meeting your challenge in a fully conscious way so that you can, perhaps, come to peace with its role in your life.

As I am reading this, I feel gratitude to you, dear body, for all the many ways you help to keep us comfortable and functional.

I notice how you are feeling right now, and I give you permission to relax as we read this, allowing these words to deeply penetrate our cellular consciousness.

Now I picture us asleep in bed tonight, knowing and understanding that you, my beloved body, will take over and put these words into action for me as I am sleeping, that I need to do nothing more than finish reading this.

I know that you know that I am feeling really challenged by _____. I would like to be able to be more comfortable dealing with this aspect of our life.

To that end, I give you permission now to release whatever seems right and appropriate for you to let go of so that we may be open to a new approach to this.

I honor you for helping me to be content with what I have and with who I am in the world.

When you reach a state where you can, with equanimity, accept whatever comes your way, you will know what it means to be truly content. When you celebrate what you have and are not just grateful for it, you will begin to embody contentment. Once you can do that you will never want for anything.

If you feel ready to take a bold step into a world where you can celebrate every aspect of your life every day, try the following assignment:

As I am reading this, I feel gratitude to you, dear body, for all the many ways you help to keep us comfortable and functional.

I notice how you are feeling right now, and I give you permission to relax as we read this, allowing these words to deeply penetrate our cellular consciousness.

Now I picture us asleep in bed tonight, knowing and understanding that you, my beloved body, will take over and put these words into action for me as I am sleeping, that I need to do nothing more than finish reading this.

I know that you know that I am sometimes less than satisfied with the life I have and that you also know that it would be possible to be not only satisfied but genuinely content with things just as they are if I were I able to banish the many thoughts that our mind generates about what is missing. I would like to have a mind that is filled with the kind of joy I sometimes feel about certain parts of my life so that I could feel that way about all of my life.

To that end, I give you permission now to release whatever seems right and appropriate to you to let go of so that we may celebrate life every day, just as it is.

I honor you for helping me to be content with what I have and with who I am in the world.

Space Clearing

As I have already mentioned, your body is every bit as much an environment as the space in which you live, making you as much of an influence on the energy of your living space as your space is on you. Ideally, your body and your living space are sacred, by which I mean that they are private spaces, respected, treasured, and protected.

But life can sometimes bring us unpleasant surprises ... and sometimes it brings those surprises right to the door.

It's time to talk about space clearing.

Actually, we've been addressing personal space clearing right along; that is what Sleep Magic is, space clearing for your internal environment. The more clear you are, the more easily your life unfolds around you. One part of Sleep Magic that we haven't mentioned yet is the acute aspect of space clearing, the times when something happens that is truly disturbing in the Now Moment, and you need to let go of whatever feelings have been generated so that they do not create new, unwanted emotional programming.

The "cure" is quick and easy, but there's a twist because you're going to want your body to let go, not only of the unwanted feeling but of whatever drew the incident to you that caused it, so that nothing like it will happen again.

Here's the formula for Sleep Magic Rescue:

As I am reading this, I allow myself to feel gratitude for all the many ways that you, my dear body, help to keep us comfortable and functional.

I notice how you are feeling, and I give you permission to relax as we are reading this, allowing the words to sink deeply into the cellular consciousness of our body.

Now I picture myself asleep in bed tonight.

I know that you remember what happened today, how it made me feel (here, if you can name the specific feeling or feelings, it's helpful). I know that you know too what lies behind our having attracted something like that to us.

So to the degree that it is comfortable for you, I give you permission to let go of that feeling (or those feelings) as well as whatever it is we are carrying that drew this situation to us.

You can fill the empty space its leaving may create by expanding the way I feel or felt (here, name a time when you were feeling something quite the opposite of what you had just experienced or simply a time when you felt peaceful).

Thank you for helping me to feel like myself again.

Onward, to your exterior living space!

You know it happens sometimes: somebody shows up at your place and they're carrying energy you wish they weren't, they're mean or they're angry, so caught up in whatever toxic situation they've drawn to themselves that for some reason they just had to share and the next thing you know they're ranting in your living room and when they leave, you can still feel it! You can feel that toxic energy hanging in the air, slowly but surely penetrating all your upholstered furniture, your drapes, even you. Help!

The remedy for an acute space clearing is quick, easy, and uncomplicated. Keep it handy! Go to your nearest gift shop—or go online—and find the highest pitched chime that you can, preferably a metal chime mounted horizontally on a wood base, (J W Stannard makes a great 'Energy Chime' in the key of a high E). Buy it, bring it home, and put it someplace handy. Much as a fire extinguisher is perfectly suited to its job, there's nothing else that can do the job of immediate-need space clearing as well as a high-pitched tone can because sound penetrates everything and breaks up that energy so fast and so well that it's as if it were never there in the first place. One good solid hit in the center of the affected room is all it takes.

For entrenched bad energies—the sort of thing you might encounter when an angry teenager finally moves out—you'll want something that incorporates actual cleaning ... and salt should be involved. Salt, a crystalline energy, absorbs anything and everything including bad energy. Sprinkle it liberally on the floor, on rugs, vacuum it up, add it to wash water. Anything you can wash, wash. Anything you can't wash, air out, outside, preferably on a sunny day. If possible, dispose of the wash water and the accumulated fuzz and dust from the vacuum outside of the house.

Note: I don't prefer sage used in interior spaces as it creates a light film on walls, much as candles do. Sage, a Native American tool for energy clearing, was designed to be used outdoors and in spaces that had a lot more airflow than do our homes today. It's a personal preference.

Here's a little more space clearing for your internal space:

As I am reading this, I allow myself to feel gratitude to you, my body, for all that you have done for me throughout the course of this day.

I notice how you are feeling, and I give you permission to relax as we are reading this, allowing the words to sink deeply into the cellular consciousness of our body.

Now I picture myself asleep in bed tonight, knowing and understanding that you, my beloved body, will take over and put these words into action for me as I am sleeping, that I need to do nothing more than finish reading this.

I know that you remember the moment that we were released from inside the warmth of our mother's body. I know we must have been startled by that, thrown into a world where our feelings of warmth and security were suddenly snatched from us. To the degree that it is comfortable for you, I give you permission to release the feelings we had at that moment.

You can fill the empty space its leaving creates by expanding the wonderful feeling of comfort that we have when we cuddle(d) up with _____.

Thank you for helping me to feel more secure within myself.

18
Detailing the Self

THE EARLY LIFE SERIES

The issue in child development is not the intentions, love or good will of the parents but the quality of the parenting environment determined by the parent's own emotional patterns—ingrained in their childhood—and by the socio-cultural economic environment.

—Gabor Maté

It takes a child 7 years to fully incarnate on the physical plane. Certain genes are switched on and other genes are switched off during this period. Thus all the future patterns of your physical health are laid down in your early years.

—Richard Rudd, from his book, *Gene Keys*

Most parents mean well. They love their children and want them to thrive. But parents are just as much the products of their cellular programming as their children are. In 1929 there was a depression that profoundly affected the lives of millions of people and went on affecting lives for generations thereafter because the people who became parents during that time produced children who were profoundly aware—over-aware—of the role that money plays in life, an awareness that became a part of who they were as adults, an awareness that was passed on easily and effortlessly to their children who were born with a cellular-based fear—an inborn sense of lack—that depending on their natures, turned into what we like to call blind ambition for some or into simply giving up for others. It is that fear of lack that has fueled the American consumer society, based almost solely now on material wealth and possessions. It had been the greed of a few, born of fear, that spawned the depression in the first place, and from there it spread like a virus.

It is no one's fault that they carry information like that. As children we have no way either to recognize or to block that information from becoming a part of who we are. As humanity evolves, so too does our self-awareness, but our grandparents were farther down that ladder than are we; generations ago, self-awareness was not on anybody's radar. We are fortunate to live at a time when self-awareness is supported and encouraged because through observation of ourselves we can not only change how we are, but we can also create an atmosphere to pass on to others that is rich with benefit. This is how we change the world, one person at a time, by changing ourselves. We can use our self-awareness to undo the very unconscious transmissions that brought us to this place and to wake us up into altering our own cellular programming consciously that we may reshape the culture in which we live from one that is based on fear and shame to one that is based on love and acceptance.

The following targeted assignments can be used by anyone. Even if you have not completed the foundational work in *Sleep Magic: Surrender to Success* (the Life Before Life Series and the Caretaker Assignments), the following assignments will be of service to you. They will establish the beginning of a relationship between you and your body, and they will initiate a process of the gradual release of some of your oldest and most deeply seated emotional programming. These foundational assignments, like those in the original Sleep Magic book which go back to the womb, are designed (metaphorically speaking) to sweep the floor before you mop it, clearing out longstanding, deeply entrenched, unconscious emotional programming thereby allowing future assignments based on more recent events to go deeper than they might otherwise.

Memories and sudden insights that may come to mind, generated by the stimulation of your cellular consciousness, should not be ignored (especially if the memories are trouble-some). Reframe the feelings that surface from a troublesome memory as follow-up assignments, giving your body permission to release whatever may have caused those bad feelings if it needs to before moving on to the next assignment in the series. Walk with the information that makes you feel good and notice if the good feelings stick around through the day. If it feels especially wonderful, you might also consider a follow-up assignment to expand the good feeling. *(You will find the follow-up assignments at the end of the Early Life Series.)*

Try not to analyze or overthink any flashes of insight; simply put them to use as the basis for a follow-up assignment or, if you are a Sleep Magic veteran, use them as a basis for a conversation with your body—more on that in a later chapter. As with the Life Before Life and Caretaker assignments from *Sleep Magic: Surrender to Success*, consider doing the Early Life series again in another eighteen months or so. Repeating the foundational assignments can be very helpful, particularly if you are feeling stuck. Because all Sleep Magic assignments are designed to allow your body to release only what it is comfortable letting go of, repeating them after a break of weeks or even months gives the body both a sense of comfort and an opportunity to let go at continually deeper levels.

You cannot overdo a Sleep Magic assignment as long as you spread out the repetition of it over time: ten to fourteen days when dealing with current, acute issues, and once a month for chronic, longstanding issues that are more likely to be rooted in your distant past.

ONE YEAR OLD

At the age of one—in fact, clear up to the age of seven—what happens to our mother may as well be happening to us. We are, for all intents and purposes, one being that consists of a mother and a child. In ancient Chinese medicine when a child under the age of seven was ill, the mother received treatment. This energetic phenomena is especially strong during the time of life when a child is unable to do anything on its own and cannot, therefore, have any sense of independence at all.

Crying Goes Unheard—Fear

As I am reading this, I allow myself to feel gratitude to you, my wonderful body, for everything you do for me every day, breathing, circulating my blood and lymph, allowing the food I eat to nourish me, protecting me.

I notice how you are feeling and give you permission to relax as we read this, allowing these words to deeply penetrate your consciousness.

Now I picture myself asleep in bed tonight, knowing and understanding that you, my beloved body, will take over and put these words into action for me as I am sleeping, that I need to do nothing more than finish reading this.

I know that you know how we may have felt afraid when we were an infant and were alone, with no one to get us for what seemed like a very long time. If any of that feeling remains anywhere inside us, I give you permission, to the degree that you are comfortable, to let it go.

You can fill any empty space that may be created by expanding the way we felt when _____ (someone came to help you when you needed it, no matter how small the incident).

Thank you for helping us both to feel more comfortable in the world.

165

Crying Goes Unheard—Feeling Alone

As I am reading this, I allow myself to feel gratitude to you, my wonderful body, for everything you do for me every day, breathing, circulating my blood and lymph, allowing the food I eat to nourish me, protecting me.

I notice how you are feeling and give you permission to relax as we read this, allowing these words to deeply penetrate your consciousness.

Now I picture myself asleep in bed tonight, knowing and understanding that you, my beloved body, will take over and put these words into action for me as I am sleeping, that I need to do nothing more than finish reading this.

I know that you know how we felt when we were an infant and were crying, alone, and no one came to get us for what seemed like a very long time. If any of that feeling remains anywhere inside us, I give you permission, to the degree that you are comfortable, to let it go.

You can fill any empty space that may be created by expanding the way we felt when _____ (someone came to help you when you needed it, no matter how small the incident).

Thank you for helping us both to feel more comfortable in the world.

Fear—General

As I am reading this, I allow myself to feel gratitude to you, my wonderful body, for everything you do for me every day, breathing, circulating my blood and lymph, allowing the food I eat to nourish me, and for protecting me.

I notice how you are feeling and give you permission to relax as we read this, allowing these words to deeply penetrate your consciousness.

Now I picture myself asleep in bed tonight, knowing and understanding that you, my beloved body, will take over and put these words into action for me as I am sleeping, that I need to do nothing more than finish reading this.

I know that you remember when we were an infant that some of those things that may have happened around us were not so good. So I give you permission now, to the degree that you are comfortable, to release any feelings of fear that we may have taken on at that time. You can fill any empty space that may be created by that release by expanding the feelings of fun I had when _____.

Thank you for helping us both to be more comfortable in the world.

Sadness

As I am reading this, I allow myself to feel gratitude to you, my body, for all that you have done for me throughout the course of this day.

I notice how you are feeling and give you permission to relax as we read this, allowing these words to deeply penetrate your consciousness.

Now I picture myself asleep in bed tonight, knowing and understanding that you, my beloved body, will take over and put these words into action for me as I am sleeping, that I need to do nothing more than finish reading this.

I know that you remember when we were an infant that some of those things that may have happened around us were not so good. So I give you permission now, to the degree that you are comfortable, to release any feelings of sadness that may have come to us then. You can fill any empty space that may be created by expanding the feelings of happiness I get/got when _____.

I honor you for helping me, for helping us, to experience more happiness in our world.

Disappointment

As I am reading this, I allow myself to feel gratitude to you, my body, for all that you have done for me throughout the course of this day.

I notice how you are feeling and give you permission to relax as we read this, allowing these words to deeply penetrate your consciousness.

Now I picture myself asleep in bed tonight, knowing and understanding that you, my beloved body, will take over and put these words into action for me as I am sleeping, that I need to do nothing more than finish reading this.

I know that you remember when we were an infant that some of those things that may have happened around us were not so good. So I give you permission now, to the degree that you are comfortable, to release any feelings of disappointment that may have come to us then. You can fill any empty space that may be created by expanding the feelings of validation I get / got when _____.

I honor you for helping me, for helping us, to experience more happiness in our world.

Anger

As I am reading this, I allow myself to feel gratitude to you, my wonderful body, for everything you do for me every day, breathing, circulating my blood and lymph, allowing the food I eat to nourish me, protecting me.

I notice how you are feeling and give you permission to relax as we read this, allowing these words to deeply penetrate your consciousness.

Now I picture myself asleep in bed tonight, knowing and understanding that you, my beloved body, will take over and put these words into action for me as I am sleeping, that I need to do nothing more than finish reading this.

I know that you remember when we were an infant that some of those things that may have happened around us were not so good. So I give you permission now, to the degree that you are comfortable, to release any feelings of unresolved or repressed anger that may have come into us at that time and to fill any empty space that may be created by expanding the pure love I have received from _____.

I honor you for helping me to love myself more and more every day.

Hopelessness

As I am reading this, I allow myself to feel gratitude for all the many ways you help to keep us comfortable and functional.

I notice how you are feeling and give you permission to relax as we read this, allowing these words to deeply penetrate your consciousness.

Now I picture myself asleep in bed tonight, knowing and understanding that you, my beloved body, will take over and put these words into action for me as I am sleeping, that I need to do nothing more than finish reading this.

I know that you remember when we were an infant that some of those things that may have happened around us were not so good. So I give you permission now, to the degree that you are comfortable, to release any feelings of hopelessness that may have come into us at that time. You can fill any empty space that may be created by expanding the feelings I got when I knew—really knew—that something was about to get better.

I honor you for helping me to be the best me I can be.

Helplessness

As I am reading this, I allow myself to feel gratitude for all the many ways you help to keep us comfortable and functional.

I notice how you are feeling and give you permission to relax as we read this, allowing these words to deeply penetrate your consciousness.

Now I picture myself asleep in bed tonight, knowing and understanding that you, my beloved body, will take over and put these words into action for me as I am sleeping, that I need to do nothing more than finish reading this.

I know that you remember when we were an infant that some of those things that may have happened around us were not so good. So I give you permission now, to the degree that you are comfortable, to release any feelings of helplessness that may have come into us at that time. You can fill any empty space that may be created by expanding the feelings I had (or have) when I felt in control of my life.

I honor you for helping me to be the best me I can be.

(If you have never felt in control of your life, consider creating an assignment around that feeling because the fact is, that there are things—like the thoughts you generate—that you can very much be in control of. By using an assignment to expand that knowing—the knowing that in that area of your life you do have control—you can improve your overall outlook.)

Guilt

The following assignment is predicated on the possibility of an infant having heard conversations in which he or she was the "cause" of something happening or not happening. Now, a one-year-old can never "cause" much of anything but with a lot of directed energy flying around, and words that are designed to induce guilt, such as, "Well, before the baby came ..." an infant—with a consciousness totally open and vulnerable—could certainly, unconsciously, take it on.

As I am reading this, I allow myself to feel gratitude to you, my body, for all that you have done for me throughout the course of this day.

I notice how you are feeling and give you permission to relax as we read this, allowing these words to deeply penetrate your consciousness.

Now I picture myself asleep in bed tonight, knowing and understanding that you, my beloved body, will take over and put these words into action for me as I am sleeping, that I need to do nothing more than finish reading this.

I know that you remember when we were an infant that some of those things that may have happened around us were not so good. So I give you permission now, to the degree that you are comfortable, to release any feelings of guilt that may have come into us from any source and to fill whatever empty space may be created by expanding the feeling of relief I had one time when I realized that something was not my fault.

Thank you for helping me to find greater peace of mind.

Worthlessness

As I am reading this, I allow myself to feel gratitude to you, my wonderful body, for everything you do for me every day, breathing, circulating my blood and lymph, allowing the food I eat to nourish me, protecting me.

I notice how you are feeling right now, and I give you permission to relax as we are reading this, allowing the words to sink deeply into the cellular consciousness of our body.

Now I picture myself asleep in bed tonight, knowing and understanding that you, my beloved body, will take over and put these

words into action for me as I am sleeping, that I need to do nothing more than finish reading this.

I know that you remember when we were an infant that some of those things that may have happened around us were not so good. So I give you permission now, to the degree that you are comfortable, to release any feelings of worthlessness that may have come into us. You can fill any empty space that may be created by expanding the feeling I get when I _____ (something that makes you feel valued).

Thank you for helping me to be everything I came here to be. I love you!

Feelings of Lack

As I am reading this, dear body, I allow myself to feel gratitude for all the many ways you help to keep us comfortable and functional.

I notice how you, my wonderful body, are feeling, and I give you permission to relax as we read this, allowing the words to sink deeply into the cellular consciousness of our body.

Now I picture myself asleep in bed tonight, knowing and understanding that you, my beloved body, will take over and put these words into action for me as I am sleeping, that I need to do nothing more than finish reading this.

I know that you remember when we were an infant that some of those things that may have happened around us were not so good. So I give you permission now, to the degree that you are comfortable, to release any feelings of lack that may have come into us from growing inside our mother and to fill the empty space by expanding the feelings I get when I enjoy beautiful things.

Thank you for helping us to be more open to all the support that we have in our lives. I honor you for helping me.

A Need to "Be Strong"

As I am reading this, I allow myself to feel gratitude for all the many ways you, dear body, help to keep us comfortable and functional.

I notice how you, my wonderful body, are feeling, and I give you permission to relax as we read this, allowing these words to sink deeply into our cellular consciousness.

Now I picture myself asleep in bed tonight, knowing and understanding that you, my beloved body, will take over and put these words into action for me as I am sleeping, that I need to do nothing more than finish reading this.

I know that you remember when we were an infant that some of those things that may have happened around us were not so good. So I give you permission now, to the degree that you are comfortable, to release any feelings of "having to be strong" that may have come into us. You can fill any empty space that may be created by expanding the feeling of release that I get when I break (or have broken) into tears.

Thank you for helping us to be more open to the support that we have in our lives. I honor you for helping me.

Helplessness

As I am reading this, I allow myself to feel gratitude to you, my wonderful body, for everything you do for me every day, breathing, circulating my blood and lymph, allowing the food I eat to nourish me, protecting me.

I notice how we are feeling right now, and I give you permission to relax as we read these words, allowing them to sink deep into our consciousness.

Now I picture myself asleep in bed tonight, knowing and understanding that you, my beloved body, will take over and put these

words into action for me as I am sleeping, that I need to do nothing more than finish reading this.

I know that you remember when we were an infant that some of those things that may have happened around us were not so good. So I give you permission now, to the degree that you are comfortable, to release any feelings of helplessness that may have come into us. You can fill any empty space that may be created by expanding the feelings I get when I know that I am being especially competent at what I am doing.

Thank you for helping me to feel good about being me. I honor you for helping me.

Resentment

As I am reading this, I allow myself to feel gratitude to you, my wonderful body, for everything you do for me every day, breathing, circulating my blood and lymph, allowing the food I eat to nourish me, protecting me.

I notice how you are feeling right now and give you permission to relax as we read this.

Now I picture myself asleep in bed tonight, knowing and understanding that you, my beloved body, will take over and put these words into action for me as I am sleeping, that I need to do nothing more than finish reading this.

I know that you remember when we were an infant that some of those things that may have happened around us were not so good. So I give you permission now, to the degree that you are comfortable, to release any feelings of resentment that may have come into us at that time. You can fill whatever empty space may be created by expanding the feelings I get when I feel especially pleased about something that has happened for me.

Thank you for helping me to be everything I came here to be. I love you!

Physical Trauma

As I am reading this, I allow myself to feel gratitude for all the many ways you, my dear body, help to keep us comfortable and functional.

I notice how you, my wonderful body, are feeling, and I give you permission to relax as we read this, allowing the words to sink deeply into the cellular consciousness of our body.

Now I picture myself asleep in bed tonight, knowing and understanding that you, my beloved body, will take over and put these words into action for me as I am sleeping, that I need to do nothing more than finish reading this.

I know that you remember when we were an infant that some of those things that may have happened to us or around us were not so good. So I give you permission now, to the degree that you are comfortable, to let go of any physical trauma we experienced at that time. You can fill any empty space that may be created by expanding the way I feel when I _____. (Here, ideally, choose something possibly very primal but definitely very physical that you really enjoy.)

I honor you for helping me. Thank you!

Doubt

As I am reading this, I allow myself to feel gratitude to you, my wonderful body, for everything you do for me every day, breathing, circulating my blood and lymph, allowing the food I eat to nourish me, protecting me.

I notice how my body is feeling right now, and I give you permission to relax as we are reading this, allowing the words to sink deeply into the cellular consciousness of our body.

Now I picture myself asleep in bed tonight, knowing and understanding that you, my beloved body, will take over and put these words into action for me as I am sleeping, that I need to do nothing more than finish reading this.

I know that you remember when we were an infant that some of those things that may have happened to us or around us were not so good. It is possible that there may at times have been an atmosphere of doubt that might have become a part of our cellular programming; if that is the case, I give you permission now, to the degree that you are comfortable, to release any doubt that may still be with us.

You can fill the empty space their leaving may create by expanding the confidence I feel/felt when I've been quite certain about something.

Thank you for helping me to feel stronger and more confident in the world!

Emotional Trauma

As I am reading this, I allow myself to feel gratitude to you, my body, for all that you have done for me throughout the course of this day.

I notice how you are feeling and give you permission to relax as we read this, allowing these words to deeply penetrate your consciousness.

Now I picture myself asleep in bed tonight, knowing and understanding that you, my beloved body, will take over and put these words into action for me as I am sleeping, that I need to do nothing more than finish reading this.

I know that you remember when we were an infant that some of those things that may have happened to us or around us were not so good. If there was anything that caused a great deal of emotional upheaval around us in that first year of our life, you have my permission tonight, to the degree that it is comfortable for you, to release any remnants of such a trauma.

You can fill the empty space their leaving creates by expanding the wonderful feeling we have when we _____.

Thank you for helping me to become more comfortable in life.

Overheard Conversations—Fear

As I am reading this, I allow myself to feel gratitude to you, my wonderful body, for everything you do for me every day, breathing, circulating my blood and lymph, allowing the food I eat to nourish me, protecting me.

I notice how you are feeling right now, and I give you permission to relax as we are reading this, allowing the words to sink deeply into the cellular consciousness of our body.

Now I picture myself asleep in bed tonight, knowing and understanding that you, my beloved body, will take over and put these words into action for me as I am sleeping, that I need to do nothing more than finish reading this.

I know that you remember conversations that happened around me when I was an infant that I have no conscious memory of. I know that I must have heard things that scared me sometimes. I know now, intellectually, that those conversations were about the people having them so I give you permission to let go of any old feelings of fear that I may have acquired in that way and to expand my own strong sense of personal safety to fill up that space.

Thank you for helping me to be everything I came here to be. I love you!

Overheard Conversations—Reduction of Self-Esteem

As I am reading this, dear body, I allow myself to feel gratitude for all the many ways you help to keep us comfortable and functional.

I notice how you, my wonderful body, are feeling, and I give you permission to relax as we are reading this, allowing the words to sink deeply into the cellular consciousness of our body.

Now I picture myself asleep in bed tonight, knowing and understanding that you, my beloved body, will take over and put these

words into action for me as I am sleeping, that I need to do nothing more than finish reading this.

I know that you remember conversations that happened around me when I was an infant that I have no conscious memory of. I know that I must have heard things that made me feel bad about myself. I know now, intellectually, that those conversations were about the people having them so I give you permission to let go of any old feelings of worthlessness I may have acquired in that way and to expand the confidence I now have in myself to fill up that space.

In the morning when I awaken I will take note of how I feel. I honor you for helping me.

Expanding the Feeling of Being Cared For

As I am reading this, I allow myself to feel gratitude for everything you, my beloved body, have done for me today.

I notice how you are feeling right now, in this moment, and I give you permission to relax as we are reading this, allowing the words to sink deeply into the cellular consciousness of our body.

Now I picture myself asleep in bed tonight, knowing and understanding that you, my beloved body, will take over and put these words into action for me as I am sleeping, that I need to do nothing more than finish reading this.

I know that you would remember the feeling of someone holding us gently, of us feeling safe and cared for. To the degree that it is comfortable for you I give you permission to release whatever is needed to allow you to expand that feeling for us, for me, so that it becomes an even bigger part of who I am.

Thank you for helping me to feel safe and secure in the world.

TWO YEARS OLD

For the first year of life we are infants; nothing is expected of us. And while we certainly take in a lot of information about our world—all of which is duly recorded in our neural circuitry and the cellular intelligence of our bodies—not much is demanded of us. But once we start walking and talking our world changes; we become potential adults and are treated as such. Yet we still carry that sense of Spirit that we are born with and it is strong. Spirit can do as it likes, but our small, newly embodied selves don't realize that there's a difference between things we can do in our surrounding environment and things we can't do, yet we're expected to grasp that. It is a challenging time for all concerned.

Overwhelm

As I am reading this, I allow myself to feel gratitude for all that you, my beloved body, have done for me in the course of the last day.

I notice how we are feeling, and I give you permission to relax as we read this, allowing the words to deeply penetrate into our cellular consciousness.

Now I picture us asleep in bed tonight; I imagine us resting comfortably.

I know that you know far better than my current consciousness knows how we were feeling when we were in our second year of life. It may be that at that time it was difficult for us to reconcile the information we brought in with us with the so-called reality that we were experiencing and that we may have been/felt overwhelmed by life experiences.

If that was the case, to the degree that you are comfortable, I give you permission to release any feelings of being overwhelmed that I may still be holding onto from that time.

You can fill the empty spaces that are created by their leaving by expanding the energy of comfort that I feel/felt when _____.

Thank you for helping me to feel happier and healthier and to function more efficiently.

Confusion

As I am reading this, I allow myself to feel gratitude for all that you, my beloved body, have done for me in the course of the last day.

I notice how we are feeling, and I give you permission to relax as we read this, allowing the words to deeply penetrate into our cellular consciousness.

Now I picture us asleep in bed tonight; I imagine us resting comfortably.

I know that you know far better than my current consciousness knows how we were feeling when we were in our second year of life. It may be that at that time it was difficult for us to reconcile the information we brought in with us with the so-called reality that we were experiencing and that we may have been/felt confused by life experiences.

If that was the case, to the degree that you are comfortable, I give you permission to release any feelings of confusion that I may still be holding onto from that time.

You can fill the empty spaces that are created by their leaving by expanding the energy of clarity that I feel/felt when _____.

Thank you for helping me feel happier and healthier and to function more efficiently.

Hearing NO

As I am reading this, I allow myself to feel gratitude for all that you, my beloved body, have done for me in the course of the last day.

I notice how we are feeling, and I give you permission to relax as we read this, allowing the words to deeply penetrate into our cellular consciousness.

Now I picture us asleep in bed tonight, imagine us resting comfortably.

I know that when we were young we heard the word "NO" far more than we heard the word "yes," because all children do.

To the degree that you are comfortable, I give you permission to release whatever feelings I may still be holding onto that are associated with having heard "NO" so many times as a child.

You can fill the empty spaces that are created by its leaving by expanding the energy of (joy, happiness, excitement, whatever) that I feel/felt when _____. (Someone gave you a thumbs-up, an enthusiastic approval, or a very heartfelt "Yes!")

Thank you for helping me to feel happier, more positive, and more sure of myself.

Helplessness

As I am reading this, I allow myself to feel gratitude for all that you, my beloved body, have done for me in the course of the last day.

I notice how we are feeling, and I give you permission to relax as we read this, allowing the words to deeply penetrate into our cellular consciousness.

Now I picture us asleep in bed tonight; I imagine us resting comfortably.

I know that you know far better than my current consciousness knows how we were feeling when we were in our second year of life. It may be that at that time I experienced a feeling of helplessness about some things that happened around me but which I was unable to stop or change.

If that was the case, to the degree that you are comfortable, I give you permission to release any feelings of helplessness that I may still be holding onto from that time.

You can fill the empty spaces that are created by their leaving by expanding the feeling of being effective that I have/had when _____.

Thank you for helping me to feel more in charge of my life.

Anger

As I am reading this, I allow myself to feel gratitude for all that you, my beloved body, have done for me in the course of the last day.

I notice how we are feeling, and I give you permission to relax as we read this, allowing the words to deeply penetrate into our cellular consciousness.

Now I picture us asleep in bed tonight; I imagine us resting comfortably.

I know that you know far better than my current consciousness knows how we were feeling when we were in our second year of life. It may be that at that time I experienced anger about some things that happened around me but was unable to express that anger.

If that was the case, to the degree that you are comfortable, I give you permission to release any feelings of anger that I may still be holding onto from that time.

You can fill the empty spaces that are created by their leaving by expanding the feeling of peace that I have/had when _____.

Thank you for helping me to feel more peaceful.

Overheard Conversations—Fear

As I am reading this, I allow myself to feel gratitude to you, my wonderful body, for everything you do for me every day, breathing, circulating my blood and lymph, allowing the food I eat to nourish me, protecting me.

I notice how you are feeling right now, and I give you permission to relax as we are reading this, allowing the words to sink deeply into the cellular consciousness of our body.

Now I picture myself asleep in bed tonight, knowing and understanding that you, my beloved body, will take over and put these words into action for me as I am sleeping, that I need to do nothing more than finish reading this.

I know that you remember conversations that happened around me when I was two that I have no conscious memory of. I know that I must have heard things that scared me sometimes. I know now, intellectually, that those conversations were about the people having them so I give you permission to let go of any old feelings of fear that I may have acquired in that way and to expand my own strong sense of personal safety to fill up that space.

Thank you for helping me to be everything I came here to be. I love you!

Overheard Conversations—Reduction of Self-Esteem

As I am reading this, dear body, I allow myself to feel gratitude for all the many ways you help to keep us comfortable and functional.

I notice how you, my wonderful body, are feeling, and I give you permission to relax as we are reading this, allowing the words to sink deeply into the cellular consciousness of our body.

Now I picture myself asleep in bed tonight, knowing and understanding that you, my beloved body, will take over and put these words into action for me as I am sleeping, that I need to do nothing more than finish reading this.

I know that you remember conversations that happened around me when I was two that I have no conscious memory of. I know that I must have heard things that made me feel bad about myself. I know now, intellectually, that those conversations were about the people having them so I give you permission to let go of any old feelings of worthlessness I may have acquired in that way and to expand the confidence I now have in myself to fill up that space.

In the morning when I awaken I will take note of how I feel. I honor you for helping me.

THREE YEARS OLD

Not too much changes in the physical world of interaction for three year olds; they are still experiencing a steep learning curve as their dexterity and mental abilities amplify. Subtle changes are taking place in the brain as the child's world ideally becomes more expectable and he or she begins to develop a sense of self. More mundane information floods the brain—the mind—and the inherent information brought in from the Spirit level of being begins to fade if it is neither mentioned nor supported by the parents.

Overwhelm

As I am reading this, I allow myself to feel gratitude for all that you, my beloved body, have done for me in the course of the last day.

I notice how we are feeling, and I give you permission to relax as we read this, allowing the words to deeply penetrate into our cellular consciousness.

Now I picture us asleep in bed tonight; I imagine us resting comfortably.

I know that you know far better than my current consciousness knows how we were feeling when we were in our third year of life. It may be that it was difficult for us to reconcile the information we brought in with us with the so-called reality that we were experiencing at the time and that we may have been/felt overwhelmed by life experiences and the growing expectations of others.

If that was the case, to the degree that you are comfortable, I give you permission to release any feelings of being overwhelmed that I may still be holding onto from that time.

You can fill the empty spaces that are created by their leaving by expanding the energy of comfort that I feel/felt when _____.

Thank you for helping me to feel more content.

Confusion

As I am reading this, I allow myself to feel gratitude for all that you, my beloved body, have done for me in the course of the last day.

I notice how we are feeling, and I give you permission to relax as we read this, allowing the words to deeply penetrate into our cellular consciousness.

Now I picture us asleep in bed tonight; I imagine us resting comfortably.

I know that you know far better than my current consciousness knows how we were feeling when we were in our third year of life. It may be that at that time it was difficult for us to reconcile the information we brought in with us with the so-called reality that we were experiencing and that we may have been/felt confused by life experiences.

If that was the case, to the degree that you are comfortable, I give you permission to release any feelings of confusion that I may still be holding onto from that time.

You can fill the empty spaces that are created by their leaving by expanding the energy of clarity that I feel/felt when _____.

Thank you for helping me to help us to feel more and more clearheaded with every passing day.

Helplessness

As I am reading this, I allow myself to feel gratitude for all that you, my beloved body, have done for me in the course of the last day.

I notice how we are feeling, and I give you permission to relax as we read this, allowing the words to deeply penetrate into our cellular consciousness.

Now I picture us asleep in bed tonight; I imagine us resting comfortably.

I know that you know far better than my current consciousness knows how we were feeling when we were in our third year of life. It may be that at that time, because I was not in control of my own life, I felt helpless.

If that was the case, to the degree that you are comfortable, I give you permission to release any feelings of helplessness that I may still be holding onto from that time.

You can fill the empty spaces that are created by their leaving by expanding the energy of being truly effective (at something, anything) that I feel/felt when _____ .

Thank you for helping me to help us feel strong in the world.

Frustration

As I am reading this, I allow myself to feel gratitude for all that you, my beloved body, have done for me in the course of the last day.

I notice how we are feeling, and I give you permission to relax as we read this, allowing the words to deeply penetrate into our cellular consciousness.

Now I picture us asleep in bed tonight; I imagine us resting comfortably.

I know that you know far better than my current consciousness knows how we were feeling when we were in our third year of life. It may be that at that time, because I was not in control of my own life and unable to physically do many things that I wanted to do that I may have felt very frustrated.

If that was the case, to the degree that you are comfortable, I give you permission to release any feelings of frustration that I may still be holding onto from that time.

You can fill the empty spaces that are created by their leaving by expanding the energy of being truly effective (at something, anything) that I feel/felt when _____.

Thank you for helping me to help us feel good in the world.

Anger

As I am reading this, I allow myself to feel gratitude for all that you, my beloved body, have done for me in the course of the last day.

I notice how we are feeling, and I give you permission to relax as we read this, allowing the words to deeply penetrate into our cellular consciousness.

Now I picture us asleep in bed tonight; I imagine us resting comfortably.

I know that you know far better than my current consciousness knows how we were feeling when we were in our third year of life. It may be that at that time I had no safe way to express the anger I would sometimes feel.

If that was the case, to the degree that you are comfortable, I give you permission to release any feelings of anger that I may still be holding onto from that time.

You can fill the empty spaces that are created by their leaving by expanding the energy of contentment that I feel/felt when _____.

Thank you for helping me to help us to feel more at peace in the world.

Overheard Conversations—Fear

As I am reading this, I allow myself to feel gratitude to you, my wonderful body, for everything you do for me every day, breathing, circulating my blood and lymph, allowing the food I eat to nourish me, protecting me.

I notice how you are feeling right now, and I give you permission to relax as we are reading this, allowing the words to sink deeply into the cellular consciousness of our body.

Now I picture myself asleep in bed tonight, knowing and understanding that you, my beloved body, will take over and put these words into action for me as I am sleeping, that I need to do nothing more than finish reading this.

I know that you remember conversations that happened around me when I was three that I have no conscious memory of. I know that I must have heard things that scared me sometimes. I know now, intellectually, that those conversations were about the people having them so I give you permission to let go of any old feelings of fear that I may have acquired in that way and to expand my own strong sense of personal safety to fill up that space.

Thank you for helping me to be everything I came here to be. I love you!

Overheard Conversations—Reduction of Self-Esteem

As I am reading this, I allow myself to feel gratitude for all the many ways you, my dear body, help to keep us comfortable and functional.

I notice how you, my wonderful body, are feeling, and I give you permission to relax as we are reading this, allowing the words to sink deeply into the cellular consciousness of our body.

Now I picture myself asleep in bed tonight, knowing and understanding that you, my beloved body, will take over and put these

words into action for me as I am sleeping, that I need to do nothing more than finish reading this.

I know that you remember conversations that happened around me when I was three that I have no conscious memory of. I know that I must have heard things that made me feel bad about myself. I know now, intellectually, that those conversations were about the people having them so I give you permission to let go of any old feelings of worthlessness I may have acquired in that way and to expand the confidence I now have in myself to fill up that space.

In the morning when I awaken I will take note of how I feel. I honor you for helping me.

FOUR YEARS OLD

Four years old is a very key time in life for more than one reason. It is the approximate cut-off time for the maximum formation of neural connections in the brain. From age four to age seven the formation of neural pathways slows down a bit and then drops off dramatically. So by four years old, the majority of our "cataloguing" of life information has been set in place. This is why, where Sleep Magic is concerned, you don't have to worry about knowing what to release as it is highly unlikely that you *would* know since most of it happened before you were four and a good deal of it happened while you were in utero.

Perhaps more importantly, the fourth year of life marks the period of life that I call **The Forgetting**. This is when the knowledge of our spiritual life and our connections to it, the knowledge of our alternate lives as humans, and our Spirit's plans for this lifetime slowly leave our consciousness, replaced by "things we need to know" to get by in the life we have chosen for ourselves. It is a huge transition of which most of our parents were likely unaware.

Anger

As I am reading this, I allow myself to feel gratitude for all that you, my beloved body, have done for me in the course of the last day.

I notice how we are feeling, and I give you permission to relax as we read this, allowing the words to deeply penetrate into our cellular consciousness.

Now I picture us asleep in bed tonight; I imagine us resting comfortably.

I know that you know far better than my current consciousness knows how we were feeling when we were in our fourth year of life. It may be that at that time I had no safe way to express the anger I would sometimes feel.

If that was the case, to the degree that you are comfortable, I give you permission to release any feelings of anger that I may still be holding onto from that time.

You can fill the empty spaces that are created by their leaving by expanding the energy of peace that I feel / felt when _____.

Thank you for helping me to help us to be more at peace in the world.

The Forgetting—Confusion

As I am reading this, I allow myself to feel gratitude for all that you, my beloved body, have done for me in the course of the last day.

I notice how we are feeling, and I give you permission to relax as we read this, allowing the words to deeply penetrate into our cellular consciousness.

Now I picture us asleep in bed tonight; I imagine us resting comfortably.

I know that you know far better than my current consciousness knows how we were feeling when we were in our fourth year of life. It may be that at that time I—we—because of all the output from others that we were exposed to, were beginning to disconnect from all the memories that we brought in with us and from the knowingness of Spirit that we carried and there may have been very real confusion around this.

If that was the case, to the degree that you are comfortable, I give you permission to release any feelings of confusion that I may still be holding onto from that time.

You can fill the empty spaces that are created by their leaving by expanding the energy of knowingness that I feel / felt when _____.

Thank you for helping me to help us to feel more clear about who we are now.

The Forgetting—Trying to Hold On—Desperation

As I am reading this, I allow myself to feel gratitude for all that you, my beloved body, have done for me in the course of the last day.

I notice how we are feeling, and I give you permission to relax as we read this, allowing the words to deeply penetrate into our cellular consciousness.

Now I picture us asleep in bed tonight; I imagine us resting comfortably.

I know that you know far better than my current consciousness knows how we were feeling when we were in our fourth year of life. It may be that at that time I—we—because of all the output from others that we were exposed to, were beginning to disconnect from all the memories that we brought in with us and from the knowingness of Spirit that we carried and we may have felt desperate to hold onto what we had known and felt as our reality.

If that was the case, to the degree that you are comfortable, I give you permission to release any feelings of desperation that we may still be holding onto from that time.

You can fill the empty spaces that are created by their leaving by expanding the energy of connection that I feel / felt when _____.

Thank you for helping me to feel more comfortable about our connections to the universal energies of which we are a part.

The Forgetting—Trying to Hold On—Sadness

As I am reading this, I allow myself to feel gratitude for all that you, my beloved body, have done for me in the course of the last day.

I notice how we are feeling, and I give you permission to relax as we read this, allowing the words to deeply penetrate into our cellular consciousness.

Now I picture us asleep in bed tonight; I imagine us resting comfortably.

I know that you know far better than my current consciousness knows how we were feeling when we were in our fourth year of life. It may be that at that time I—we—because of all the output from others that we were exposed to, were beginning to disconnect from all the memories that we brought in with us and from the knowingness of Spirit that we carried and we may have felt very sad as our connection to Spirit slipped away.

If that was the case, to the degree that you are comfortable, I give you permission to release any feelings of sadness that we may still be holding onto from that time.

You can fill the empty spaces that are created by their leaving by expanding the energy of the joy that I feel/felt now when I can sense that connection with Spirit (or with another person).

Thank you for helping me to help us know happiness in this life.

The Forgetting—Loneliness

As I am reading this, I allow myself to feel gratitude for all that you, my beloved body, have done for me in the course of the last day.

I notice how we are feeling, and I give you permission to relax as we read this, allowing the words to deeply penetrate into our cellular consciousness.

Now I picture us asleep in bed tonight; I imagine us resting comfortably.

I know that you know far better than my current consciousness knows how we were feeling when we were in our fourth year of life. It may be that at that time I—we—because of all the output from others that we were exposed to, were beginning to disconnect from not only the memories that we brought in with us but from our access to otherworldly beings and we may have begun to feel lonely as our connection to these Spirits slipped away.

If that was the case, to the degree that you are comfortable, I give you permission to release any feelings of loneliness that we may still be holding onto from that time.

You can fill the empty spaces that are created by their leaving by expanding the energy of the joy that I feel/felt now when I sense spirit energy around me (or when I am enjoying being in the company of others).

Thank you for helping me to know contentment in this life.

Overheard Conversations—Fear

As I am reading this, I allow myself to feel gratitude to you, my wonderful body, for everything you do for me every day, breathing, circulating my blood and lymph, allowing the food I eat to nourish me, protecting me.

I notice how you are feeling right now, and I give you permission to relax as we are reading this allowing the words to sink deeply into the cellular consciousness of our body.

Now I picture myself asleep in bed tonight, knowing and understanding that you, my beloved body, will take over and put these words into action for me as I am sleeping, that I need to do nothing more than finish reading this.

I know that you remember conversations that happened around me when I was four that I have no conscious memory of. I know that I must have heard things that scared me sometimes. I know now, intellectually, that those conversations were about the people having them so I give you permission to let go of any old feelings of fear that I may have acquired in that way and to expand my own strong sense of personal safety to fill up that space.

Thank you for helping me to be everything I came here to be. I love you!

Overheard Conversations—Reduction of Self-Esteem

As I am reading this, I allow myself to feel gratitude for all the many ways you, my dear body, help to keep us comfortable and functional.

I notice how you, my wonderful body, are feeling, and I give you permission to relax as we are reading this, allowing the words to sink deeply into the cellular consciousness of our body.

Now I picture myself asleep in bed tonight, knowing and understanding that you, my beloved body, will take over and put these words into action for me as I am sleeping, that I need to do nothing more than finish reading this.

I know that you remember conversations that happened around me when I was four that I have no conscious memory of. I know that I must have heard things that made me feel bad about myself. I know now, intellectually, that those conversations were about the people having them so I give you permission to let go of any old feelings of worthlessness I may have acquired in that way and to expand the confidence I now have in myself to fill up that space.

In the morning when I awaken I will take note of how I feel. I honor you for helping me.

FIVE YEARS OLD

By the time we reach five years of age we have become officially human. Our Spirit connections have been, for the most part, forgotten unless we are very fortunate indeed. At five years old we are beginning to be expected to perform many simple and basic tasks for ourselves. Some children of this age even find themselves in the structured environment of a preschool system where they are exposed to more personalities than may previously have been the case and the challenges of becoming a "social" being are met.

The sense of self by age five is crystallizing and as conversational abilities begin to expand so too do relationships at every level. At five you are a small human in a very big human world. The programming you now carry as a result of all the adult feedback you have received go on to affect your adult life and will lie at the root of job satisfaction, dissatisfaction, the ability to form commitments or not, and the lack or presence of self-confidence.

Confusion

As I am reading this, I allow myself to feel gratitude for all that you, my beloved body, have done for me in the course of the last day.

I notice how we are feeling, and I give you permission to relax as we read this, allowing the words to deeply penetrate into our cellular consciousness.

Now I picture us asleep in bed tonight; I imagine us resting comfortably.

I know that you know far better than my current consciousness knows how we were feeling when we were in our fifth year of life. It may be that at that time it was difficult for us to make the shift from being thought of and treated like a baby to finding ourselves with expectations to be met.

If that was the case, to the degree that you are comfortable, I give you permission to release any feelings of confusion that I may still be holding onto from that time.

You can fill the empty spaces that are created by their leaving by expanding the energy of clarity that I feel/felt when _____.

Thank you for helping me feel happier and healthier and to function more efficiently in my world.

Overwhelm

As I am reading this, I allow myself to feel gratitude for all that you, my beloved body, have done for me in the course of the last day.

I notice how we are feeling, and I give you permission to relax as we read this, allowing the words to deeply penetrate into our cellular consciousness.

Now I picture us asleep in bed tonight; I imagine us resting comfortably.

I know that you know far better than my current consciousness knows how we were feeling when we were in our fifth year of life. It may be that at that time it was difficult for us to make the shift from a child to that of being, essentially, a very small adult and that we may have been/felt overwhelmed by the challenges we encountered.

If that was the case, to the degree that you are comfortable, I give you permission to release any feelings of being overwhelmed that I may still be holding onto from that time.

You can fill the empty spaces that are created by their leaving by expanding the energy of comfort that I feel/felt when _____.

Thank you for helping me to feel happier and healthier and to function more efficiently.

Lack of Support for the Individual Becoming

As I am reading this, I allow myself to feel gratitude for all that you, my beloved body, have done for me in the course of the last day.

I notice how we are feeling, and I give you permission to relax as we read this, allowing the words to deeply penetrate into our cellular consciousness.

Now I picture us asleep in bed tonight; I imagine us resting comfortably.

I know that you know far better than my current consciousness knows how we were feeling when we were in our fifth year of life. This was a time when I was just beginning to have a sense of myself as a separate—and important!—being. I suspect that I may not have received the kind of feedback about my newly discovered feelings of self-worth that I'd have liked and that as a result I may have felt as if I weren't worth all that much as I'd thought.

If that was the case, to the degree that you are comfortable, I give you permission to let go of any feelings of worthlessness that we may still be holding onto from that time.

You can fill the empty spaces that are created by their leaving by expanding the feeling I had when _____ (a time that you were praised in a memorable way, even if it was only for a small thing).

Thank you for helping us to recognize and enjoy who we are in the world.

Anger at Opinions Not Being Recognized as Important

As I am reading this, I allow myself to feel gratitude for all that you, my beloved body, have done for me in the course of the last day.

I notice how we are feeling, and I give you permission to relax as we read this, allowing the words to deeply penetrate into our cellular consciousness.

Now I picture us asleep in bed tonight; I imagine us resting comfortably.

I know that you know far better than my current consciousness knows how we were feeling when we were in our fifth year of life. This was a time when I was just beginning to have a sense of myself as a separate being and a time when I began to have definite ideas of my own. I suspect that my ideas and opinions may not have been recognized as having value at that time and that I may have felt anger about that, even if I was not permitted to express it or felt that I could not.

If that was the case, to the degree that you are comfortable, I give you permission to let go of any anger that we may still be holding onto from that time.

You can fill the empty spaces that are created by their leaving by expanding the feeling I had when _____ (... such as when an idea you had—however small or insignificant—was lauded).

Thank you for helping us to recognize and enjoy who we are, as we are.

Frustration at Not Being Able to Act on Own Ideas

As I am reading this, I allow myself to feel gratitude for all that you, my beloved body, have done for me in the course of the last day.

I notice how we are feeling, and I give you permission to relax as we read this, allowing the words to deeply penetrate into our cellular consciousness.

Now I picture us asleep in bed tonight; I imagine us resting comfortably.

I know that you know far better than my current consciousness knows how we were feeling when we were in our fifth year of life. This was a time when I was just beginning to have a sense of myself as a separate being and a time when I began to have definite ideas of my own. I suspect that because my ideas and opinions may not have been recognized as having value at that time, I may not have been able to act on them and that I may have experienced some frustration with this.

If that was the case, to the degree that you are comfortable, I give you permission to let go of any frustration that we may still be holding onto from that time.

You can fill the empty spaces that are created by their leaving by expanding the feeling I had when _____ (... someone told you that it was OK to do something).

Thank you for helping us to recognize and enjoy our value in the world.

Frustration at Not Being Able to Be as Skilled as Desired

As I am reading this, I allow myself to feel gratitude for all that you, my beloved body, have done for me in the course of the last day.

I notice how we are feeling, and I give you permission to relax as we read this, allowing the words to deeply penetrate into our cellular consciousness.

Now I picture us asleep in bed tonight; I imagine us resting comfortably.

I know that you know far better than my current consciousness knows how we were feeling when we were in our fifth year of life. This was a time when I was just beginning to learn how to do things for myself. Dexterity can be a challenging skill and early learning is always a challenge so I know that things sometimes didn't go my way and that I may well have grown quite frustrated with my abilities.

If that was the case, to the degree that you are comfortable, I give you permission to let go of any task-related frustration that we may still be holding onto from that time.

You can fill the empty spaces that are created by their leaving by expanding the feeling I had when _____ (... you did something right! Any time).

Thank you for helping me to take it easy on myself sometimes.

Anger at Being Judged to Be Unskilled

As I am reading this, I allow myself to feel gratitude for all that you, my beloved body, have done for me in the course of the last day.

I notice how we are feeling, and I give you permission to relax as we read this, allowing the words to deeply penetrate into our cellular consciousness.

Now I picture us asleep in bed tonight; I imagine us resting comfortably.

I know that you know far better than my current consciousness knows how we were feeling when we were in our fifth year of life. This was a time when I was just beginning to learn how to do things for myself. Dexterity can be a challenging skill and early learning is always a challenge so I know that things sometimes didn't go my way and that despite my sincere efforts I may have experienced judgment from someone who thought that I should be doing better.

If that was the case, to the degree that you are comfortable, I give you permission to let go of any anger in response to that judgment that we may still be holding onto from that time.

You can fill the empty spaces that are created by their leaving by expanding the feeling I had when _____ (... you were congratulated on your performance. Anytime).

Thank you for helping us to recognize and be comfortable with our value in the world, just as we are.

Inborn Confidence Reduced or Destroyed

As I am reading this, I allow myself to feel gratitude for all that you, my beloved body, have done for me in the course of the last day.

I notice how we are feeling, and I give you permission to relax as we read this, allowing the words to deeply penetrate into our cellular consciousness.

Now I picture us asleep in bed tonight; I imagine us resting comfortably.

I know that you know far better than my current consciousness knows how we were feeling when we were in our fifth year of life. It may be that at that time that the innate confidence we'd been born with was slowly eroded by all the criticism and correction that we received.

If that was the case, to the degree that you are comfortable, I give you permission to release whatever seems right and appropriate to you in order to restore and expand the natural confidence that was my birthright.

Thank you for helping me to be more truly myself with each passing day.

Overheard Conversations—Fear

As I am reading this, I allow myself to feel gratitude to you, my wonderful body, for everything you do for me every day, breathing, circulating my blood and lymph, allowing the food I eat to nourish me, protecting me.

I notice how you are feeling right now, and I give you permission to relax as we are reading this, allowing the words to sink deeply into the cellular consciousness of our body.

Now I picture myself asleep in bed tonight, knowing and understanding that you, my beloved body, will take over and put these words into action for me as I am sleeping, that I need to do nothing more than finish reading this.

I know that you remember conversations that happened around me when I was five that I have no conscious memory of. I know that I must have heard things that scared me sometimes. I know now, intellectually, that those conversations were about the people having them so I give you permission to let go of any old feelings of fear that I may have acquired in that way and to expand my own strong sense of personal safety to fill up that space.

Thank you for helping me to be everything I came here to be. I love you!

Overheard Conversations—Reduction of Self-Esteem

As I am reading this, I allow myself to feel gratitude for all the many ways you, my dear body, help to keep us comfortable and functional.

I notice how you, my wonderful body, are feeling, and I give you permission to relax as we are reading this, allowing the words to sink deeply into the cellular consciousness of our body.

Now I picture myself asleep in bed tonight, knowing and understanding that you, my beloved body, will take over and put these words into action for me as I am sleeping, that I need to do nothing more than finish reading this.

I know that you remember conversations that happened around me when I was five that I have no conscious memory of. I know that I must have heard things that made me feel bad about myself. I know now, intellectually, that those conversations were about the people having them so I give you permission to let go of any old feelings of worthlessness I may have acquired in that way and to expand the confidence I now have in myself to fill up that space.

In the morning when I awaken I will take note of how I feel. I honor you for helping me.

Doubting Own Abilities

As I am reading this, I allow myself to feel gratitude to you, my wonderful body, for everything you do for me every day, breathing, circulating my blood and lymph, allowing the food I eat to nourish me, protecting me.

I notice how you are feeling right now, and I give you permission to relax as you read these words, allowing them to penetrate our cellular consciousness with ease.

Now I picture myself asleep in bed tonight, knowing and understanding that you, my beloved body, will take over and put these words into action for me as I am sleeping, that I need to do nothing more than finish reading this.

I know that you know how my struggles with learning may have caused me to doubt myself and my abilities. If any of that doubt is still hanging around, it would not be useful for either of us, so to the degree that it is comfortable for you I give you permission to release it if it is still with us.

You can fill the empty space its leaving creates by expanding the feeling I've had when I knew (something) for absolute sure with every cell in my body. (And if you never did, just give your body permission to expand whatever feels right and appropriate to it.)

Thank you for helping me to honor myself all the way down to my cells.

Parental Projections of Inadequacy

As I am reading this, I allow myself to feel gratitude for all that you, my beloved body, have done for me in the course of the last day.

I notice how we are feeling, and I give you permission to relax as we read this, allowing the words to deeply penetrate into our cellular consciousness.

Now I picture us asleep in bed tonight; I imagine us resting comfortably.

I know that you know far better than my current consciousness knows how we were feeling when we were in our fifth year of life. It may be that at that time, just as we were starting to have some more critical control over dexterity and language, that our (mother/father/both) began to see in us a mirror of their own shortcomings and projected their sense of inadequacy onto us unconsciously.

If that was the case, to the degree that you are comfortable, I give you permission to release any sense of inadequacy that I may still be holding onto from that time.

You can fill the empty spaces that are created by their leaving by expanding the energy of confidence that I feel/felt when _____. (This could be something as simple as peeling a carrot or brushing your teeth ... pick whatever it is that you feel most adept at or let your body pick for you.)

Thank you for helping me feel happier and healthier and to function more efficiently in my world.

Anger at Self for Not Doing a Good Job

As I am reading this, I allow myself to feel gratitude for all that you, my beloved body, have done for me in the course of the last day.

I notice how we are feeling, and I give you permission to relax as we read this, allowing the words to deeply penetrate into our cellular consciousness.

Now I picture us asleep in bed tonight; I imagine us resting comfortably.

I know that you know far better than my current consciousness knows how we were feeling when we were in our fifth year of life. This was a time when I was just beginning to learn how to do things for myself. Dexterity can be a challenging skill and early learning is always a challenge so I know that things sometimes didn't go my way and that I may have become frustrated and angry with myself for not performing in a way that I may have perceived to have been expected of me.

If that was the case, and we are still holding onto it, then to the degree that you are comfortable, I give you permission to let go of that anger and frustration.

You can fill the empty spaces that are created by their leaving by expanding the feeling I had when _____ (... you knew that you did something well ... anything at all).

Thank you for helping us to be satisfied with who we are, as we are.

SIX YEARS OLD

At six we begin to find ourselves more out in the world; our range of input is expanded as most of us are sent to school and enter a world of acknowledged competition (as opposed to possible unacknowledged competition at home) and vastly more opportunities for being judged and/or rejected.

Separation Anxiety

As I am reading this, I allow myself to feel gratitude to you, my wonderful body, for everything you do for me every day, breathing, circulating my blood and lymph, allowing the food I eat to nourish me, protecting me.

I notice how you are feeling right now and give you permission to relax as we read this, allowing these words to penetrate deeply into our cellular consciousness.

Now I picture myself asleep in bed tonight, knowing and understanding that you, my beloved body, will take over and put these words into action for me as I am sleeping, that I need to do nothing more than finish reading this.

I know that you remember our first days in school, how it was being away from home for a long time on my own. If I experienced any anxiety about that separation that may still be with us today, I give you permission to release it as it would serve no purpose for us.

You can fill the empty space its leaving creates by expanding the energy I feel/felt when I am with _____ (loving friends or similar in my home).

Thank you for helping me to be more comfortable in my world.

Anxiety around the Energy of Other Children

As I am reading this, I allow myself to feel gratitude to you, my wonderful body, for everything you do for me every day, breathing, circulating my blood and lymph, allowing the food I eat to nourish me, protecting me.

I notice how you are feeling right now and give you permission to relax as we read this, allowing these words to penetrate deeply into our cellular consciousness.

Now I picture myself asleep in bed tonight, knowing and understanding that you, my beloved body, will take over and put these words into action for me as I am sleeping, that I need to do nothing more than finish reading this.

I know that you remember our first days in school, how it was being in the close company of so many other children. If I experienced any anxiety around being exposed to so much other high energy of types different from what I had been used to that may still be with us today, I give you permission to release it as it would serve no purpose for us at this time.

You can fill the empty space its leaving creates by expanding the energy I feel/felt when I am _____ (in a space where I feel safe and comfortable).

Thank you for helping me to be more comfortable in my world.

Having Enthusiasm Squashed

As I am reading this, I allow myself to feel gratitude for all that you, my beloved body, have done for me in the course of the last day.

I notice how we are feeling, and I give you permission to relax as we read this, allowing the words to deeply penetrate into our cellular consciousness.

Now I picture us asleep in bed tonight; I imagine us resting comfortably.

I know that you know that there is some chance that our youthful enthusiasm may have been squashed at some point during our sixth year when we were opening up to more opportunities than we ever had so far.

If that happened, I'd like to remedy it, so I give you permission to let go of anything we might still be carrying around with us that might be telling us to ever give anything less than all we've got to things that we really want to do.

Thank you for helping me to be more available to all that the world has to offer me.

Anger at Being Judged

As I am reading this, I allow myself to feel gratitude for all that you, my beloved body, have done for me in the course of the last day.

I notice how we are feeling, and I give you permission to relax as we read this, allowing the words to deeply penetrate into our cellular consciousness.

Now I picture us asleep in bed tonight; I imagine us resting comfortably.

I know that you know far better than my current consciousness knows how we were feeling when we were in our sixth year of life. This was a time when I was expanding my skill as well as learning how to "learn," in the context of a school situation. I know that things sometimes didn't go my way and that I may have experienced what felt like judgment from someone who thought that I should be doing better.

If that was the case, to the degree that you are comfortable, I give you permission to let go of any anger in response to that judgment that we may still be holding onto from that time.

You can fill the empty spaces that are created by their leaving by expanding the feeling I had when _____ (... you were congratulated on something, anything).

Thank you for helping us to recognize and be comfortable with our value in the world, just as we are.

A Sense of Shame at Being Judged

It is one thing to be judged at home and quite another to be judged in public.

As I am reading this, I allow myself to feel gratitude for all that you, my beloved body, have done for me in the course of the last day.

I notice how we are feeling, and I give you permission to relax as we read this, allowing the words to deeply penetrate into our cellular consciousness.

Now I picture us asleep in bed tonight; I imagine us resting comfortably.

I know that you know far better than my current consciousness knows how we were feeling when we were in our sixth year of life. This was a time when I was expanding my skill as well as learning how to "learn," in the context of a school situation. I know that things sometimes didn't go my way and that I may have experienced a sense of shame when I was judged or criticized by someone who thought that I should be doing better.

If that was the case, to the degree that you are comfortable, I give you permission to let go of any shame that we may still be holding onto from that time.

You can fill the empty spaces that are created by their leaving by expanding the feeling of pride I had when _____ (... you were congratulated on your performance, anytime and for anything, however small it may seem).

Thank you for helping us to recognize and be comfortable with our value in the world, just as we are.

Feeling a Need to Hurry

As I am reading this, I allow myself to feel gratitude to you, my wonderful body, for everything you do for me every day, breathing, circulating my blood and lymph, allowing the food I eat to nourish me, protecting me.

I notice how you are feeling right now and give you permission to relax as we read this, allowing these words to penetrate deeply into our cellular consciousness.

Now I picture myself asleep in bed tonight, knowing and understanding that you, my beloved body, will take over and put these words into action for me as I am sleeping, that I need to do nothing more than finish reading this.

I know that you remember our first days in school, how many new things had to be learned and how many new things there were to do. I know that there is some chance that at that time I felt a pressure to get things done that may still be with me.

If that is the case, I give you permission to release it, as it would serve no purpose for us at this time in our life.

You can fill the empty space its leaving creates by expanding the energy I feel/felt when I am _____ (... doing something, moving comfortably, at your own speed).

Thank you for helping me to be more comfortable in my world.

Doubting Own Abilities

As I am reading this, I allow myself to feel gratitude to you, my wonderful body, for everything you do for me every day, breathing, circulating my blood and lymph, allowing the food I eat to nourish me, protecting me.

I notice how you are feeling right now, and I give you permission to relax as you read these words, allowing them to penetrate our cellular consciousness with ease.

Now I picture myself asleep in bed tonight, knowing and understanding that you, my beloved body, will take over and put these words into action for me as I am sleeping, that I need to do nothing more than finish reading this.

I know that you know how my struggles with learning may have caused me to doubt myself and my abilities. If any of that doubt is still hanging around, it would not be useful for either of us, so to the degree that it is comfortable for you I give you permission to release it if it is still with us.

You can fill the empty space its leaving creates by expanding the feeling I've had when I knew (something) for absolute sure with every cell in my body. (And if you never did, just knowing the right answer to a question will do. You can always work with what you've got!)

I honor you for helping me to feel more confident and sure of who I am and of my abilities.

Frustration at Not Living Up to Own Expectations

As I am reading this, I allow myself to feel gratitude for all that you, my beloved body, have done for me in the course of the last day.

I notice how we are feeling, and I give you permission to relax as we read this, allowing the words to deeply penetrate into our cellular consciousness.

Now I picture us asleep in bed tonight; I imagine us resting comfortably.

I know that you know far better than my current consciousness knows how we were feeling when we were in our sixth year of life. This was a time when I was expanding my skill as well as learning how to "learn," in the context of a school situation. I know that things sometimes didn't go my way and that I may have experienced some frustration with myself because I thought that I should be doing better.

If that was the case, to the degree that you are comfortable, I give you permission to let go of any shame that we may still be holding onto from that time.

You can fill the empty spaces that are created by their leaving by expanding the feeling of pride I had when _____ (… you were congratulated on your performance, anytime and for anything, however small it may seem).

Thank you for helping us to recognize and be comfortable with our value in the world, just as we are.

Parental Projections of Social Inadequacy

As I am reading this, I allow myself to feel gratitude for all that you, my beloved body, have done for me in the course of the last day.

I notice how we are feeling, and I give you permission to relax as we read this, allowing the words to deeply penetrate into our cellular consciousness.

Now I picture us asleep in bed tonight; I imagine us resting comfortably.

I know that you know far better than my current consciousness knows how we were feeling when we were in our sixth year of life. It may be that at that time, just as we were starting to expand our social circle, that our (mother/father/both) began to see in us a mirror of their own shortcomings and projected their sense of social inadequacy onto us unconsciously.

If that was the case, to the degree that you are comfortable, I give you permission to release any sense of social inadequacy that I may be holding onto from that time.

You can fill the empty spaces that are created by their leaving by expanding the energy of confidence that I feel/felt when _____ (this could be anything from having a pleasant conversation with someone or a quick and efficient pleasant exchange at a checkout).

Thank you for helping me feel happier and healthier and to function more efficiently in my world.

Feeling Different

As I am reading this, I allow myself to feel gratitude to you, my wonderful body, for everything you do for me every day, breathing, circulating my blood and lymph, allowing the food I eat to nourish me, protecting me.

I notice how you are feeling right now and give you permission to relax as we read this, allowing these words to penetrate deeply into our cellular consciousness.

Now I picture myself asleep in bed tonight, knowing and understanding that you, my beloved body, will take over and put these words into action for me as I am sleeping, that I need to do nothing more than finish reading this.

I know that you know that at six years of age, I may well have felt "different" from the other children that I met. Intellectually, I know that such a thing was logical, as these were "new" people and my sphere of contacts was expanding outside of my comfort zone but there is some chance that the emotional part of us may still be holding onto that "outsider" feeling.

So, to the degree that it is possible and comfortable for you, I give you permission to let go of such feelings if they are still with us.

You can fill the empty space its leaving creates by expanding the energy I feel/felt when I am _____ (with someone in particular from any time in life or with a group that I feel very much at one with).

Thank you for helping me to be more comfortable in my world.

Overheard Conversations—Fear

As I am reading this, I allow myself to feel gratitude to you, my wonderful body, for everything you do for me every day, breathing, circulating my blood and lymph, allowing the food I eat to nourish me, protecting me.

I notice how you are feeling right now, and I give you permission to relax as we are reading this, allowing the words to sink deeply into the cellular consciousness of our body.

Now I picture myself asleep in bed tonight, knowing and understanding that you, my beloved body, will take over and put these words into action for me as I am sleeping, that I need to do nothing more than finish reading this.

I know that you remember conversations that happened around me when I was six that I have no conscious memory of. I know that I must have heard things that scared me sometimes. I know now, intellectually, that those conversations were about the people having them so I give you permission to let go of any old feelings of fear that I may have acquired in that way and to expand my own strong sense of personal safety to fill up that space.

Thank you for helping me to be everything I came here to be. I love you!

Overheard Conversations—Reduction of Self-Esteem

As I am reading this, dear body, I allow myself to feel gratitude for all the many ways you help to keep us comfortable and functional.

I notice how you, my wonderful body, are feeling, and I give you permission to relax as we are reading this, allowing the words to sink deeply into the cellular consciousness of our body.

Now I picture myself asleep in bed tonight, knowing and understanding that you, my beloved body, will take over and put these words into action for me as I am sleeping, that I need to do nothing more than finish reading this.

I know that you remember conversations that happened around me when I was six that I have no conscious memory of. I know that I must have heard things that made me feel bad about myself. I know now, intellectually, that those conversations were about the people having them so I give you permission to let go of any old feelings of worthlessness I may have acquired in that way and to expand the confidence I now have in myself to fill up that space.

In the morning when I awaken I will take note of how I feel. I honor you for helping me.

Follow-up Assignment Format

Thank you, dear body, for all the work you did for me today. I am so grateful for breathing and for my blood circulating, for digesting food and casting off what we do not need.

I notice how my body is feeling right now, as I read this.

Now I picture myself asleep in bed tonight, knowing and understanding that you, my beloved body, will take over and put these words into action for me as I am sleeping, that I need to do nothing more than finish reading this.

I know that you know what lay behind the way I felt when I awoke this morning. I give you permission to release, to the degree that it is comfortable for you, whatever caused that. You can then fill the empty space that is created by expanding the feeling of _____ (some feeling that is as opposite as you can find from the one being released) that I experienced _____.

I honor you for helping me to become clearer with each passing day.

Expanding Good Feelings

Thank you, dear body, for all the work you did for me today. I am grateful for our breathing and for our blood circulating, for digesting food and casting off what we do not need.

I notice how you, my body, are feeling right now, as I read this, and I give you permission to relax as we read these words.

Now I picture myself asleep in bed tonight, knowing and understanding that you, my beloved body, will take over and put these words into action for me as I am sleeping, that I need to do nothing more than finish reading this.

I know that you know how good I felt when I awoke this morning (or during a dream state, or anytime!). Our life would benefit greatly if it were filled with even more of such good feelings, so I give you permission to release, to the degree that it is comfortable for you, whatever might seem unnecessary or unneeded and also feels appropriate in order that you might expand the energy of those good feelings.

Thank you for helping us to more fully enjoy life.

IN CONCLUSION

The key to making the most of this book is not just to use it, but to use it so much and so often that it allows the assignment process to become a part of your daily life, that it allows you to open a dialogue with your body that is ongoing and not just based on you wanting to fix your life but on you wanting what is best both for you and your body. Developing a respectful and communicative relationship with your body will bring you a more comfortable life; it's that simple.

Ideally, you will begin not only thanking your body throughout the day for the many tasks it performs for you, delighting with it in satisfying bowel movements, the taste of good food, deep belly breathing, and countless other mundane happenings that you experience throughout the day but also turning the assignment format itself into caring and respectful conversations that may happen on the spur of a moment.

Once you reach that point, you will probably discover that your body will be acting on your words on the spot, as if it were holding up its own end of the conversation, granting you what you require almost as soon as the words have left your consciousness. You will find that your body will no longer need sleep to get your Ego Process tucked safely out of the way.

I wish you well!

About the Author

Victoria Pendragon was born and raised in the vicinity of Philadelphia, Pennsylvania. She is the oldest of eleven. Her life has been defined, as are most of ours perhaps, by conditions that would seem to have been beyond her control. Eighteen years of various sorts of abuse and two diseases that should have killed her rank among the most outstanding of those.

Her study of metaphysics began in early childhood as an attempt to validate the lessons she'd been learning from the earth and the trees whenever she left her body. She has been working as a professional in the field of spirituality since 1995, has read tarot since 1964.

Victoria began training in art when still a child, eventually acquiring a BFA from The Philadelphia College of Art. Her work hangs in numerous corporate and personal collections, among them The Children's Hospital of the University of Pennsylvania, Moss Rehabilitation Center and Bryn Mawr Rehabilitation Hospital.

She has two children by her first marriage, a son and a daughter, both of whom amaze her. She is currently married to her third husband, a man whose kind soul has created for her an atmosphere of clarity and creativity in which she dances, writes, creates art and helps when asked.

Books by Victoria Pendragon

Feng Shui From the Inside, Out
Published by: Ozark Mountain Publishing

Sleep Magic
Published by: Ozark Mountain Publishing

The Grail: A Beginners Guide to Spiritual Realization, Self-Actualization & Metaphysics
On 8 CDs, Self-Published

My Three Years as A Tree
Self-Published

The Little Chakra Book
Self-Published

For more information about any of the above titles, soon to be released titles, or other items in our catalog, write, phone or visit our website:
Ozark Mountain Publishing, LLC
PO Box 754, Huntsville, AR 72740
479-738-2348/800-935-0045
www.ozarkmt.com

If you liked this book, you might also like:

Dancing on a Stamp
by Garnet Schulhauser
Soul Speak
by Julia Cannon
Soul Choices: Six Paths to Find Your Life Purpose
by Kathryn Andries
Sit A Bit
by Victor Parachin
Evolution of the Spirit
by Walter Pullen
Let's Get Natural with Herbs
by Debra Rayburn
Ask Your Inner Voice
by James Wawro

For more information about any of the above titles, soon to be released titles,
or other items in our catalog, write, phone or visit our website:
Ozark Mountain Publishing, LLC
PO Box 754, Huntsville, AR 72740
479-738-2348
www.ozarkmt.com

Other Books By Ozark Mountain Publishing, Inc.

Dolores Cannon
A Soul Remembers Hiroshima
Between Death and Life
Conversations with Nostradamus,
    Volume I, II, III
The Convoluted Universe -Book One,
    Two, Three, Four
The Custodians
Five Lives Remembered
Jesus and the Essenes
Keepers of the Garden
Legacy from the Stars
The Legend of Starcrash
The Search for Hidden Sacred Knowledge
They Walked with Jesus
The Three Waves of Volunteers and the
    New Earth
Aron Abrahamsen
Holiday in Heaven
Out of the Archives – Earth Changes
Justine Alessi & M. E. McMillan
Rebirth of the Oracle
Kathryn/Patrick Andries
Naked In Public
Kathryn Andries
The Big Desire
Dream Doctor
Soul Choices: Six Paths to Find Your Life
    Purpose
Soul Choices: Six Paths to Fulfilling
    Relationships
Tom Arbino
You Were Destined to be Together
Rev. Keith Bender
The Despiritualized Church
O.T. Bonnett, M.D./Greg Satre
Reincarnation: The View from Eternity
What I Learned After Medical School
Why Healing Happens
Julia Cannon
Soul Speak – The Language of Your Body
Ronald Chapman
Seeing True
Albert Cheung
The Emperor's Stargate
Jack Churchward
Lifting the Veil on the Lost Continent of Mu
The Stone Tablets of Mu
Sherri Cortland
Guide Group Fridays
Raising Our Vibrations for the New Age
Spiritual Tool Box
Windows of Opportunity
Cinnamon Crow
Chakra Zodiac Healing Oracle
Teen Oracle
Michael Dennis
Morning Coffee with God

God's Many Mansions
Claire Doyle Beland
Luck Doesn't Happen by Chance
Jodi Felice
The Enchanted Garden
Max Flindt/Otto Binder
Mankind: Children of the Stars
Arun & Sunanda Gandhi
The Forgotten Woman
Maiya & Geoff Gray-Cobb
Angels -The Guardians of Your Destiny
Seeds of the Soul
Julia Hanson
Awakening To Your Creation
Donald L. Hicks
The Divinity Factor
Anita Holmes
Twidders
Antoinette Lee Howard
Journey Through Fear
Vara Humphreys
The Science of Knowledge
Victoria Hunt
Kiss the Wind
James H. Kent
Past Life Memories As A Confederate
    Soldier
Mandeep Khera
Why?
Dorothy Leon
Is Jehovah An E.T
Mary Letorney
Discover The Universe Within You
Sture Lönnerstrand
I Have Lived Before
Irene Lucas
Thirty Miracles in Thirty Days
Susan Mack & Natalia Krawetz
My Teachers Wear Fur Coats
Patrick McNamara
Beauty and the Priest
Maureen McGill & Nola Davis
Live From the Other Side
Henry Michaelson
And Jesus Said – A Conversation
Dennis Milner
Kosmos
Guy Needler
Avoiding Karma
Beyond the Source – Book 1, Book 2
The History of God
The Origin Speaks
James Nussbaumer
The Master of Everything
Sherry O'Brian
Peaks and Valleys
Riet Okken
The Liberating Power of Emotions

Other Books By Ozark Mountain Publishing, Inc.

John Panella
The Gnostic Papers
Victor Parachin
Sit a Bit
Nikki Pattillo
A Spiritual Evolution
Children of the Stars
Rev. Grant H. Pealer
A Funny Thing Happened on the
  Way to Heaven
Worlds Beyond Death
Karen Peebles
The Other Side of Suicide
Victoria Pendragon
Feng Shui from the Inside, Out
Sleep Magic
Walter Pullen
Evolution of the Spirit
Christine Ramos, RN
A Journey Into Being
Debra Rayburn
Let's Get Natural With Herbs
Charmian Redwood
A New Earth Rising
Coming Home to Lemuria
David Rivinus
Always Dreaming
Briceida Ryan
The Ultimate Dictionary of Dream
  Language
M. Don Schorn
Elder Gods of Antiquity
Legacy of the Elder Gods

Gardens of the Elder Gods
Reincarnation...Stepping Stones of Life
Garnet Schulhauser
Dancing Forever with Spirit
Dancing on a Stamp
Annie Stillwater Gray
Education of a Guardian Angel
Blair Styra
Don't Change the Channel
Natalie Sudman
Application of Impossible Things
Dee Wallace/Jarrad Hewett
The Big E
Dee Wallace
Conscious Creation
James Wawro
Ask Your Inner Voice
Janie Wells
Payment for Passage
Dennis Wheatley/ Maria Wheatley
The Essential Dowsing Guide
Jacquelyn Wiersma
The Zodiac Recipe
Sherry Wilde
The Forgotten Promise
Stuart Wilson & Joanna Prentis
Atlantis and the New Consciousness
Beyond Limitations
The Essenes -Children of the Light
The Magdalene Version
Power of the Magdalene
Robert Winterhalter
The Healing Christ

For more information about any of the above titles, soon to be released titles,
or other items in our catalog, write, phone or visit our website:
PO Box 754, Huntsville, AR 72740
479-738-2348/800-935-0045
www.ozarkmt.com